Short Bike Rides™
in and around Philadelphia

Short Bike Rides™

in and around

Philadelphia

Ann Lembo
and
Joe Surkiewicz

An East Woods Book

The
Globe
Pequot
Press

Old Saybrook, Connecticut

Library of Congress Cataloging-in-Publication Data

Lembo, Ann.
   Short bike rides in and around Philadelphia / Ann Lembo and Joe
Surkiewicz — 1st ed.
         p.   cm.
      "An East Woods book."
      ISBN 1-56440-073-5
      1. Bicycle touring—Pennsylvania—Philadelphia Region—Guidebooks.
   2. Philadelphia Region (Pa.)—Guidebooks. I. Surkiewicz, Joe.
   II. Title
GV1045.5.P4L46 1993   93-48965
796.6'4'0974811—dc20   CIP

♻ This text is printed on recycled paper
Manufactured in the United States of America
First Edition/Second Printing

To our moms

About the Authors

Ann Lembo began her love affair with bikes as a youngster exploring the Bucks County roads around her home in Levittown, Pennsylvania. Today she rides her road, mountain, and tandem bikes near Baltimore, Maryland, where she's a student at the University of Maryland School of Law.

Her best friend and biking buddy, Joe Surkiewicz, is a freelance reporter and author. His latest book is *The Unofficial Guide to Washington, D.C.*, published by Prentice Hall Travel/Simon & Schuster. He's also the author of *The Mountain Biker's Guide to Central Appalachia*, published by Menasha Ridge/Falcon Press. He's an avid road and mountain cyclist and a frequent contributor to *Mountain Biking*, *VeloNews*, *Dirt Rag*, and *Spokes*.

Acknowledgments

Thanks to the many people who assisted us in researching and writing this book. Every government agency and park we contacted was helpful in supplying information, maps, and advice. In particular, we'd like to thank Philippe Crist at the Rails to Trails Conservancy in Washington, John Wood at the Montgomery County Planning Commission for his help on the Schuylkill Trail, Fawn and Brad Kiddle at Kiddle Cyclery in Buckingham for their help in Bucks County, and some of the many friendly Philadelphia-area cyclists we met while riding: Ernie Bloom, Carol Guerrero, and Adam Singer. Thanks for your insights, directions, and advice.

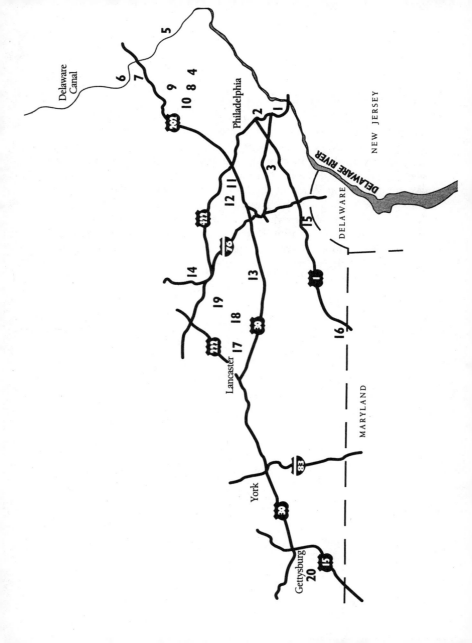

Contents

Introduction

Say the word *Philadelphia* and most people think of the Liberty Bell, Benjamin Franklin, and cheese steak hoagies. And that's pretty good imagery for evoking the spirit of America's fourth largest city, located on the Delaware River. After all, our country's foremost symbol of freedom, a towering genius of the eighteenth century, and scrumptious food sum up this city fairly well.

Yet we think there's another item folks should add to this list of symbols that represent the City of Brotherly Love: a bicycle.

Why? With its wealth of historical sites, long-settled neighborhoods featuring honest-to-God colonial homes, natural beauty, and gentle terrain, Philadelphia and its environs are perfect for bicyclists who thrill to the feel of the wind in their faces and the power of their legs as they tour by bike. From Independence National Historical Park in center-city Philadelphia, home of Independence Hall and the Liberty Bell Pavilion, to beautiful Fairmount Park, at 8,900 acres the largest urban park in the United States, downtown Philly offers two-wheeled tourists a wealth of fascinating locales to explore.

But that's not all that awaits bicyclists who explore this majestic city by bike—not by a long shot. Outside the city limits suburban Philadelphia tempts bike riders with the lush, opulent countryside of Bucks, Chester, Delaware, and Montgomery counties, where cyclists spin down pretty country lanes lined with fieldstone mansions and beautiful estates. Before, after, and during a ride, cyclists can stop in restored villages and inns to shop, grab a bite to eat, and soak up the well-heeled ambience. In the spring flowers bloom along the narrow roads and the air is heavy with the sweet smell of honeysuckle. In the fall trees that create a canopy over the lanes erupt in a riot of red, yellow, and orange.

Let there be no doubt about it—Philadelphia and the rolling, picturesque countryside around it add up to a world-class cycling destination.

But if gorgeous country vistas aren't enough to entice you to grab your bike and explore beyond the city's limits, then how about an intimate history lesson about America's past? Within an hour's drive of center-city, bicyclists can explore sites that played crucial roles in the formation of our country.

At Valley Forge, located about 20 miles west of Philadelphia, cyclists can explore the encampment where General George Washington and his ragtag army endured the cold winter of 1777–78. Inside the park a paved bike trail leads riders across rolling, well-kept grounds and past reconstructed log huts, artillery emplacements, and monuments.

Southwest of Philadelphia, folks on bikes can explore Brandywine Battlefield State Park, where British forces defeated Washington before occupying the young nation's new capital, Philadelphia.

The park is also a great starting point for an easy and fun-filled ride along the meandering Brandywine River. The route takes you past horse farms and colonial-era stone houses, barns, and walls. Other sights you'll see on the ride include Longwood Gardens, a former DuPont estate and one of the best formal gardens in the United States, and the Brandywine River Museum, home of paintings by the Wyeth family and other American masters.

On a historical up-note, cyclists will thrill to Washington Crossing State Park, where Washington and his army crossed the Delaware River to begin a successful attack against British forces in New Jersey. Then they can take a cruise on the Delaware and Raritan (D&R) Canal Trail, a towpath that features flat, scenic riding along this magnificent river.

As we researched this book, local cyclists we met on rides urged us to include two wildly popular cycling areas that aren't, strictly speaking, in the Philadelphia area: Lancaster County and Gettysburg. Their arguments were compelling—both locales are acclaimed by local riders for unsurpassed natural beauty. We agree that they should be on any bicyclist's list of great Philadelphia destinations. And they're both within a day's drive.

Lancaster County, about 50 miles west of the city on U.S. 30, is arguably one of the best cycling destinations in the world. Featuring neat-as-a-pin Amish farms; narrow, low-traffic roads; and gorgeous rolling countryside, Lancaster County offers cyclists hundreds of miles of great riding. We include three of the best Lancaster County rides in this book.

Farther west, Gettysburg National Military Park, located in south-central Pennsylvania about 130 miles from Philadelphia, treats two-wheeled visitors to a double whammy: spectacular history on the site where Union forces in 1863 reversed the tide of the Civil War in the largest battle ever fought in the Western Hemisphere—and some of the most pleasant rural bike riding in the United States. Don't miss it.

With the surge of popularity in mountain bikes (fat-tired bicycles with upright handlebars, beefy frames and brakes, and ultralow gearing), we feel no guide to Philadelphia-area rides would be complete without a few great off-road riding destinations. True, most people can and do ride their fat-tired bikes (and their not-so-fat-tired cousins, hybrid bikes) on paved roads. But one of the attractions of owning a mountain bike is exercising the option to escape every cyclist's nemesis: traffic. How? By riding your mountain bike on paved bike paths, dirt roads, and trails. And the Philadelphia area has a wealth of parks with miles of off-road routes to choose from.

One of the best off-road destinations you'll find is, ironically enough, in downtown Philadelphia: Fairmount Park. Starting at the Philadelphia Museum of Art (its grand neoclassical facade immortalized in the *Rocky* movies), fat-tired cyclists can explore a paved path along the Schuylkill River that passes boathouses, statues, beautiful parklands, mansions, and great views of the river and downtown Philadelphia. It's hard to believe this oasis of sylvan tranquillity dominates America's fourth largest city.

Connecting to the trails in Fairmount Park is the Schuylkill Trail, a 22-mile paved bikeway that follows the Schuylkill River, a tributary of the Delaware River, upstream to Valley Forge. Along the way cyclists are treated to river views and a minicourse in American industrial history.

Only a short drive north of Philadelphia on the New Jersey side of the Delaware River, the D&R Canal entices fat-tired cyclists with scenic riverside riding and the chance to explore restored villages that specialize in antiques, inns, restaurants, and charm. In nearby Tyler State Park, mountain bikers shift into ultralow gears to ride paved trails through a hilly woodlands preserve in rapidly developing Bucks County. To the west in Chester County, two county-owned parks, Hibernia and Nottingham, welcome mountain bikers to their miles of hiking trails and dirt roads, while Ridley Creek State Park offers a delightful 5-mile bike path that's paved and traffic-free. Mountain bikers looking for more challenging riding (meaning steep climbs and twisting trails) can find it at French Creek State Park, located about 40 miles west of Philadelphia.

History, beautiful rolling countryside, a wealth of places to ride away from traffic—Philadelphia has it all for folks who thrill to two-wheel exploration. As you survey these twenty rides, keep in mind that many can serve as jumping-off points for more extensive tours; in fact, several of the rides overlap and can be combined for longer rides. Each route is accompanied by a map that lists the starting point, suggested direction of travel, street names, and attractions.

If you're a novice cyclist, or someone who's just getting into the sport, here are a few pointers that will help you get the most out of bicycling—and this book.

Bikes

Today the most popular bicycle by far is the mountain bike. Featuring a great ride, rugged construction, and very low gears, mountain bikes (also called all terrain bikes, or ATBs) account for nearly two-thirds of all new bicycle sales. What makes mountain bikes the number one seller? In a nutshell, people love their stable ride and upright riding position.

Another bike style that's coming on strong is the hybrid bike, also known as the fitness or city bike. While at first glance it looks like a mountain bike, the hybrid is usually lighter and sports narrower tires and bigger wheels than mountain bikes. It's a compromise bike for folks who like the feel of a mountain bike but don't plan to do a lot of off-road riding. Other varieties include racing bikes (with skinny tires and drop handlebars), touring bikes (similar to racing models but set up for a more comfortable ride and carrying panniers), and tandems.

So which style is best? No one but you can answer that question.

4

Here's some advice: If you're in the market for a new bike, visit your local bike shop. Unlike most department and hardware stores, bike shops are staffed by people who care about cycling. They'll put you on a bike that matches your riding style, fits properly, and is correctly assembled and adjusted when you take it home.

Helmets

Let's be clear about this: Unlike, say, skydiving or rock climbing, bicycling is *not* an inherently dangerous activity. Yet we feel that after purchasing a bike, the number one accessory every cyclist should buy is a helmet. Personal experience has taught us that wearing a helmet can save your life—or prevent you from living it out in a vegetative state. With today's comfortable, lightweight models and low prices (around $40), there's no excuse not to wear one.

Safety

Cyclists riding the public highways have both the rights and the responsibilities of drivers. Ride with the flow of traffic, stay as far to the right as is practical and safe, and signal your turns. And keep in mind that most car/bike accidents occur at intersections, so that's where you need to be the most alert. Off-road riders should always keep their speed under control and yield to hikers and equestrians.

Regarding personal safety, all the rides in this book are located in relatively safe areas. But since violent crime can happen anywhere, try to ride with at least one companion, especially on urban rides. Another defense is to be in good shape, usually not a problem for cyclists: In a threatening situation, sprint.

If you're harassed by an obnoxious motorist, try to stay calm, while noting the car's license plate number, model, and color. Also, try to get a look at the driver's face. Then get to a private home, pay phone, or business and call the police. Remember, you have a right to the road (with obvious exceptions, such as interstates) as much as a car driver does, and anyone who verbally abuses or threatens you is breaking the law. Report that person to the police.

Things to Take on a Ride

By carrying a few spare parts and tools on a ride, you'll extend the sense of self-sufficiency that makes cycling such a blast. You'll also avoid the humiliation of calling home for a ride if you break down. Items you should pack include a spare tube, a patch kit and tire irons, a pump, one or more water bottles, an adjustable wrench, a small screwdriver, a set of allen wrenches (2–6 mm), something to eat, and some money (at least enough change for a phone call or a soda). If you plan to park your bike, even for a moment, bring a lock.

Folks who venture off-road should carry one additional item in their bag of tricks: a chain tool, a lightweight item used to remove the bike's chain. Here's why: Loose sticks on the trail have a way of jamming rear derailleurs and breaking them in half, reducing your twenty-one-speed mountain bike to a zero-speed version that's good only for coasting down hills. While it's a rare event, it usually happens miles from the trailhead. That's when a chain tool is worth its weight in gold: You can break the chain, take out a few links, and reassemble it so that your bike is now a one-speed, which means you can ride, instead of walk, to your car or home.

Fairmount Park

Mileage:	8
Approximate pedaling time:	1 hour
Terrain:	Flat
Traffic:	None, except where the bike path crosses entrances to parking lots
Things to see:	Scullers on the Schuylkill River, beautiful manicured parklands and gardens, the Philadelphia Museum of Art, Boathouse Row, Boelsen Cottage (circa 1660), stately mansions overlooking the river
Directions at a glance:	From the Philadelphia Museum of Art (there's plenty of parking behind it), ride north along the east side of the river (the path follows Kelly Drive) for about 4 miles. Cross the river on Falls Bridge and follow the bike path south along the west side of the river. Take the bridge over the river near the museum to return to your car.

What an unusual park! With 8,900 acres of winding creeks, rustic trails, lush green meadows, and 100 miles of jogging, bicycling, and bridal paths, Philadelphia's Fairmount Park is the largest landscaped city park in the world.

Yet Fairmount Park isn't unique just because of its size and urban setting. It also has a rich history, as well as proximity to the beloved icons of America's past.

Consider: Fairmount Park was the site of the Centennial Exposition of 1876, a glorious fair that celebrated America's hundredth birthday with an eye-popping display of industrial might and ingenuity. Today this vast collection of Victorian technology is on exhibit in the Smithsonian Arts and Industry Building, located on the National Mall in Washington, D.C.

In nearby center-city Philadelphia is "America's most historic square mile"—literally America's birthplace. **Independence Hall** (where the Declaration of Independence was adopted and the U.S. Constitution was written), the **Liberty Bell Pavilion, Declaration House** (where Thomas Jefferson drafted the Declaration of Independence), **Christ Church** (an active parish since 1695)—these treasure-houses of American history and more are only a short distance from Fairmount Park. To visit them by bike without battling a lot of car and truck traffic, go early in the morning on a weekend or holiday before a ride in Fairmount Park. Head down Benjamin Franklin Parkway (the broad boulevard in front of the **Philadelphia Museum of Art**) to City Hall, then go east on Market Street.

Even closer is the **Philadelphia Museum of Art**, perhaps best known for its marvelous facade, put to good use in the *Rocky* movies. Inside you'll find such treasures as Marcel Duchamp's *Nude Descending a Staircase*—one of 300,000 art pieces on display in America's third largest art museum. Here's a tip: Admission to the museum is usually $5.00, but on Sundays it's free from 10:00 A.M. to 1:00 P.M.

Fairmount Park's natural beauty, its proximity to some of America's richest historical sites, and an adjacent world-class art museum are all excellent reasons to visit this urban jewel. But to really enjoy Fairmount Park, explore it on a bicycle.

Taking advantage of the plentiful parking behind the **Philadelphia Museum of Art**, two-wheel visitors can easily park their cars and depart on an effortless ramble that takes them along both banks of the Schuylkill River.

One thing's for sure: You won't be alone.

Bicyclists of all stripes and breeds flock to Fairmount Park: Mountain bikers, road racers in colorful jerseys and slick black tights, and casual riders out for a leisurely spin crowd the many miles of bike

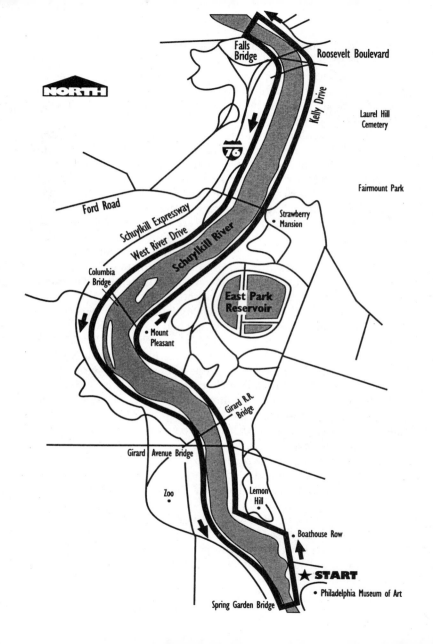

paths that wind through the park. And that's in addition to the walkers, joggers, and in-line skaters who flock to Fairmount Park year-round. On the river you can usually see scullers and racing eights training for a race.

Here's an easy ride that will introduce you to some of the best sights in Fairmount Park. Start behind the **Philadelphia Museum of Art** (its back faces the river) and ride on the bike path that commences near the bike rental shop. In the spring azalea gardens on the drive past **Boathouse Row** are ablaze in brilliant reds and oranges. Guarding nearby **Fairmount Waterworks** are statues of six Revolutionary War heroes that are among 200 pieces of sculpture dotting the park. **Boathouse Row,** a group of classic Tudor structures, is home to the "Schuylkill Navy"—Philadelphia's famous rowing clubs.

Riding north along the east side of the river on the bike path bordering Kelly Drive (named after Olympic rowing champion John, brother to Grace), cyclists are treated to views of the river, manicured lawns, statues, and monuments. Plenty of benches and picnic tables make it easy to stop and soak it in.

Above the Girard Street Bridge and across Kelly Drive, look for Frederic Remington's *Cowboy,* the sculptor's only large-scale work. Three sculpture plazas along the river depict the founding of the nation and its development. All are worth the time to stop, read the inscriptions, and linger—easily done on a bike.

As you continue north, the park gets a little wider—and, usually, a little less crowded. Along the way you'll pass the **Boat Race Stands** and, across Kelly Drive, the entrances to **Lemon Hill, Mount Pleasant, Laurel Hill,** and **Strawberry Mansion,** four of seven restored eighteenth- and nineteenth-century mansions that were the homes of prominent Philadelphians.

At Falls Bridge turn left to cross the river for the return leg of the ride along the west bank. Traffic is usually lighter along West River Drive, but you pay a price: The bike path is bumpier where tree roots push the asphalt up. Come to think of it, a fat-tired mountain bike might be the perfect choice for this ride!

Continuing south, views of the city slowly unfold ahead of you. Look for the **Boelsen Cottage,** built in the 1660s, just across West

River Drive. Along the way there's an exercise route where you can make periodic stops and get an upper-body workout.

Soon, after passing the low dam in the river across from the classically styled **Waterworks**, you swing across the river and, bearing left, ride around the museum and back to your car.

What's next? A suggestion: Following this dose of natural beauty, contrast it with a stroll through the Philadelphia Museum of Art for a sampling of the works of great artists.

For Further Information

Philadelphia Visitors Center (800) 537–7676 or (215) 636–1666

Getting There

From I–95 take the Vine Street Expressway west and get on the Ben Franklin Parkway, which ends at the Philadelphia Museum of Art. From the Schuylkill Expressway (I–76), exit at Thirtieth Street and follow the signs to the museum.

Schuylkill Trail

Mileage:	21.5
Approximate pedaling time:	2 to 2.5 hours, one way
Terrain:	Flat
Traffic:	None
Things to see:	River views, rural countryside, nineteenth-century industrial architecture, a canal towpath and restored canal locks, the Philadelphia skyline, the Philadelphia Museum of Art
Directions at a glance:	No directions are needed to ride the bikeway. The trail can be ridden out and back or, by parking a car at the other end, as a one-way ride.

When most of us take the trouble of loading the bikes on the car and heading out to a favorite cycling destination, it's to escape the pressures of urban and suburban life—the congestion, traffic, and crowded landscape that are the reality of late-twentieth-century life. We seek rural byways, bucolic scenery, and the near-isolation afforded by bicycling away from the city and through uncrowded farmland, forests, and countryside. It's a way of recharging our batteries.

Yet you don't always need to drive beyond the city limits to find quiet cycling routes. With the tremendous success of the rails-to-trails movement—the process of claiming abandoned railroad lines and converting them into "linear parks" for use by cyclists, hikers, and other nonmotorized recreational users—a growing number of urban and suburban paths are now available for exploration. One of the most successful of the new trails is the Schuylkill Trail, which fol-

lows the river of the same name from center-city Philadelphia to Valley Forge, 18 miles northwest of the city.

While the trail offers cyclists plenty of river views, chances to see wildlife, and sections of rural countryside, it features a lot more: glimpses into America's industrial past, preserved throughout the ancient river valley for two-wheeled travelers who take the time to explore this fascinating stretch of paved trail.

Along the way you'll see several centuries of human development on display: the remains of river and canal navigation, evidence of limestone and iron ore quarrying, iron and steel production, and railroad transportation. More recent development along the route includes high-rise urban renewal in the boroughs of Conshohocken and Norristown. Like an archaeologist on an urban dig, you'll discover layer after layer of human activity on a leisurely ramble along the Schuylkill Trail.

Going west to east from the Betzwood end of the trail (near Valley Forge), you'll pass other attractions, including Synthane Taylor, once the site of a film studio where 1930s and 1940s western movies were filmed. Barbadoes Island is a wildlife refuge that's owned by the Philadelphia Electric Company and marked by twin smokestacks from an old coal-fired electric plant. **Riverfront Park** in Norristown is a great resting or picnic spot, while the town itself offers fine examples of nineteenth-century architecture, as well as river vistas.

The bikeway next passes through deep cuts exposing soluble limestone and dolomite rock formations and then goes behind the former Alan Wood Steel Works, just north of Conshohocken. The Washington Fire Company Building in Conshohocken has been in continual use since 1874 and features Italian-style architecture. Today it is surrounded by the first of the town's new riverside developments.

In the village of Spring Mill, cyclists are treated to sights of homes dating from the late 1700s. From the **Manayunk Canal Towpath**, you'll see Flat Rock Dam and restored canal locks. Closer to center-city, cyclists ride through scenic Fairmount Park.

Both ends of the trail offer additional areas ripe for exploration by adventurous cyclists. **Valley Forge National Historic Park** features a 6.5-mile paved bike path through the rolling countryside where

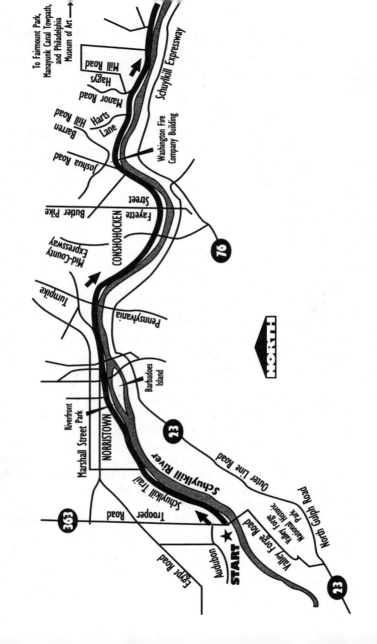

George Washington and the Grand Army wintered in 1777–78. There is also a lovely, 2.5-mile scenic riverside walking trail that connects to Pawlings Road. Eventually the Schuylkill Trail will continue beyond **Valley Forge Park** on the rail corridor, across the river, and to the park's visitor center.

In downtown Philadelphia **Fairmount Park** offers folks on bikes grand views of the Schuylkill River, the city's striking skyline, numerous pieces of sculpture, and stately mansions as you pedal along West River Drive and Kelly Drive. The imposing **Philadelphia Museum of Art** marks the eastern end of the Schuylkill Trail.

For natural beauty and a lesson in the region's industrial history, a ride along the Schuylkill Trail offers cyclists a lot. And with its convenient location, it's an easy way to recharge those batteries!

For Further Information

Montgomery County Planning Commission (215) 278–3736.

Getting There

Park at either terminus of the trail: Betzwood, on Pennsylvania 422 near **Valley Forge National Historic Park**, or behind the **Philadelphia Museum of Art** in center-city. Additional parking along the trail can be found at **Riverfront Park** in Norristown and near the trail in Conshohocken, Spring Mill, and Manayunk.

Ridley Creek State Park

Mileage:	5
Approximate pedaling time:	1 hour
Terrain:	Gently rolling
Traffic:	None
Things to see:	**Hunting Hill, the Colonial Pennsylvania Plantation** (a living museum of a Delaware County Quaker farm circa 1776), beautiful woodlands and meadows
Directions at a glance:	No directions are needed to ride the 5-mile bike trail.

Encompassing 2,606 acres of rolling woodlands and meadows in the heart of suburban Delaware County, Ridley Creek State Park is a mecca for Philly-area cyclists who like leisurely riding away from the hassles of traffic. In addition to a 5-mile bike trail that makes a loop through the park, folks on two wheels can ride low-traffic, low-speed paved roads throughout the park. It's the perfect destination for those whose legs—and maybe rear ends—cry out for relief from the flat riding in **Fairmount Park** and the **Schuylkill Trail**.

First, some history: The park is on the site of a small eighteenth-century village that's now known as Sycamore Mills but was also named Bishop's Mill and Upper Providence Corn Mill. Visitors can see the miller's house, the office and library, and several small mill-workers' dwellings from the old village. And don't miss the impressive mansion that serves as today's park office: **Hunting Hill**, built in 1914, is a stone structure situated on well-manicured grounds.

Another not-to-be-missed sight inside the park is the **Colonial**

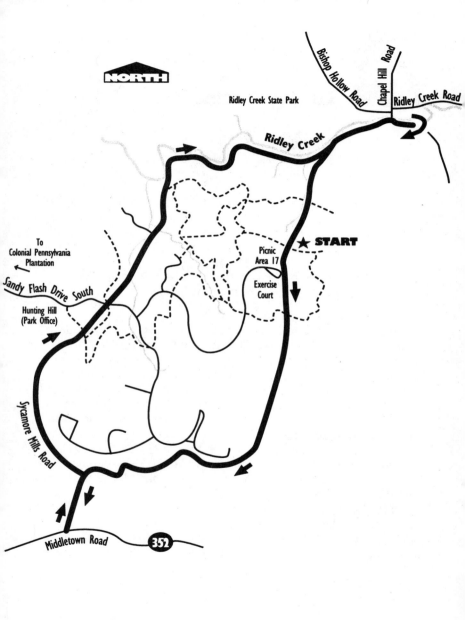

Pennsylvania Plantation, a working farm for nearly 300 years. Historical interpreters give visitors an accurate picture of farm life on a 1776 Quaker farm—as do a variety of farm animals and an authentic landscape. The plantation is open April through November on weekends, 10:00 A.M. to 4:00 P.M. An admission fee is charged.

To reach parking for the bike trail, follow signs inside the park to picnic area 17 and the exercise court. You can park your car in the cul-de-sac and begin riding on the 20-foot-wide paved trail visible through the line of trees. Watch your speed as you spin along the trail; cyclists share the route with walkers, runners, in-line skaters, and family groups with small children.

While both skinny- and fat-tired bikes are suitable for riding on the bike trail, keep in mind that mountain bikes are *not* allowed on the 17 miles of hiking and equestrian trails located in Ridley Creek State Park. Stick to riding the pavement and you'll be OK.

For Further Information

Ridley Creek State Park (215) 566–4800

Getting There

Located only 16 miles from center-city Philadelphia, Ridley Creek State Park's entrance is on Pennsylvania 3, 2.5 miles west of Newtown Square.

Tyler State Park

Mileage:	10.5
Approximate pedaling time:	2 hours
Terrain:	Hilly
Traffic:	None
Things to see:	The longest covered bridge in Bucks County, beautiful forests and pristine streams, old stone buildings dating back to the eighteenth century
Directions at a glance:	No specific directions are needed for this ride, although a suggested route is outlined below. As you enter the park, stop at the Ranger Office and pick up a map. Bicycling is permitted on paved areas only.

Pack up the kids and bring the whole family to Tyler State Park, a little island of greenery amid the sprawling suburbs of Bucks County. It's an oasis of forests, streams, pre–Revolutionary War Americana, and agricultural activity. And don't forget the bikes!

First, though, some history: After all, these rolling hills weren't always surrounded by tract houses, mini-estates, and convenience stores.

Originally inhabited by the Leni-Lenape Indians, the land in this area was sold to William Penn on June 23, 1682, at nearby Council Rocks. Later Penn subdivided the land into smaller plots and sold them to early colonists. (Nearby Levittown, with acres of ticky-tacky houses on tiny lots, shows what happens when subdividing gets out of hand.)

Today the park comprises 1,711 acres of woodlands and fields that have been carefully preserved in their pristine glory. Original

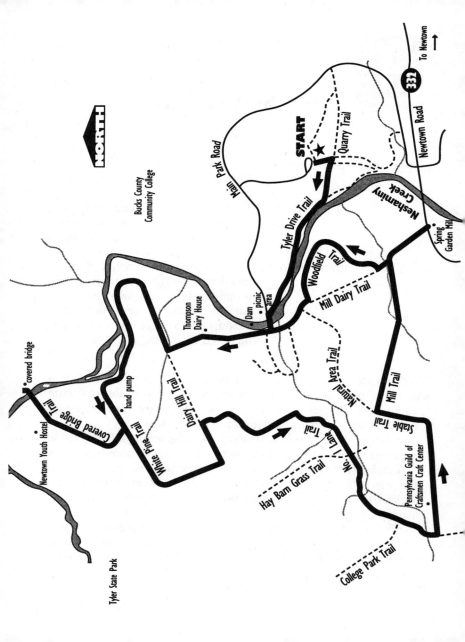

stone buildings, some dating back to the early 1700s, have also been preserved and are maintained by private individuals currently leasing the buildings.

Neshaminy Creek winds throughout the park, separating the woodlands from the parking and commercial area. The creek also serves as park boundary in some places.

Here's a suggestion for a Tyler State Park bicycle ramble: After entering the park from Pennsylvania 332, drive to the first parking area past the Ranger Office. Park here and ride your bicycle to the Quarry Trail, which winds through the picnic grove and then connects with Tyler Drive Trail.

This scenic route follows the banks of the Neshaminy Creek to the concession area, which is open seven days a week from Memorial Day weekend through Labor Day.

As you ride along Neshaminy Creek, keep an eye out for wildlife: Snapping turtles, frogs, and water snakes are just a few of the animals that make their home here. Did you bring a fishing rod? The creek harbors sunnies, black crappie, carp, smallmouth bass, and other pan fish.

After crossing Neshaminy Creek on the pedestrian causeway near the concession area, you leave the bustle and crowds and plunge back into the woods. Turn right on the Mill Dairy Trail, which leads past the Thompson Dairy House, built in 1775. Although you can get close enough to read the date stone, this historic building is not open to the public.

Continue past the dairy house to the next intersection and turn right. Now you're headed back toward the creek, and the trail follows the banks of the Neshaminy. As the trail heads west, you'll climb up toward one of the many picnic areas scattered throughout the park. Look for a handpump for water, take a break, and refill your water bottle.

At the picnic site the Dairy Hill Trail intersects with the Covered Bridge Trail on the right. Going straight, the former becomes the White Pine Trail; take the Covered Bridge Trail down past the Newtown Youth Hostel.

The hostel, located in the Solly house and annex, provides rustic hotel service for travelers on foot or bicycle. It's part of a network of more than 200 hostels that supply overnight accommodations where visitors share chores, bring their own gear, and clean up after themselves.

The hostel's buildings were the original farm buildings and were used by Mr. and Mrs. George F. Tyler (who purchased the land that was later to become the park) while waiting for their mansion to be built. Today the mansion is part of Bucks County Community College, adjacent to the park.

Farther downhill is a pleasant surprise: the longest covered bridge in Bucks County. Once you've ridden across, you'll discover that the road disappears: It's a great area to explore by mountain bike.

The bridge is located at a beautiful spot on the banks of Neshaminy Creek that is also a great place to take a break. Afterward, retrace your route uphill on Covered Bridge Trail. This is quite a steep hill, so take it slow and easy.

Now turn right onto White Pine Trail. True to its name, the trail winds through a white pine stand toward the western edge of the park. The trail ends back at the Dairy Hill Trail; turn left.

Next turn right on No. 1 Lane Trail, which leads past another picnic area and parallels some of the park's equestrian trails. This area of mature hardwoods is intersected with small streams that help to water the thriving understory of blackberry, spicebush, and jewelweed.

Continuing on, the trail goes through deep woods (despite the paved surface)—though you'll catch an occasional glimpse of farmfields. Surprise: One-quarter of the park is under cultivation, and crops include winter wheat, feed corn, soybeans, and hay. The next intersection is with College Park Trail, which goes off to the right and is an out-and-back trail through the same woods leading to the park boundary.

No. 1 Lane Trail continues as a wonderfully level footpath with farmfields to the right. Soon you'll pass a parking lot on your right. A left leads to the Pennsylvania Guild of Craftsmen Craft Center.

Just past the craft center, pick up the Stable Trail, then turn right onto Mill Trail, which goes to the old Spring Garden Mill. This building was taken over by the Langhorne Players, a local theater group, to be developed into a theater for its productions.

Mill Trail intersects with Newtown Road (Pennsylvania 332),

which leads out of the park. Unless you're leaving the park, turn around, climb the hill, and continue on to the Mill Dairy Trail.

To the right is the Woodfield Trail, a loop that leads past another picnic area and through some beautiful woods along the ridge: Take it. The leaves from the oaks growing along the ridge have turned the soil acidic, making ideal growing conditions for maple viburnum, mountain laurel, and wintergreen.

Woodfield Trail intersects with the Mill Dairy Trail again, where you can turn right to continue back to the pedestrian causeway or stay awhile to explore some of the other trails in the park.

When's the best time to visit Tyler State Park? In spring the forest is exploding with new life, while in summer the leafy canopy offers respite from the heat of the sun. In fall the leaves begin to change in October, and the crisp, cool air of autumn is great for riding. Winter, while usually cold, offers great views from the hilltops to the rolling countryside beyond the park's borders.

In other words, any time is a good time to visit this natural oasis located in the center of Bucks County's suburban sprawl!

For Further Information

Bucks County Historical–Tourist Commission (215) 752–2203
Tyler State Park (215) 968–2021
Newtown Youth Hostel (215) 968–0927

Getting There

Tyler State Park is off exits 27 and 28 of the Pennsylvania Turnpike. From exit 27 follow Pennsylvania 332 east from Willow Grove through Richboro. From exit 28 follow U.S. 1 north to I–95; follow I–95 north to the Newtown-Yardley exit; and drive west on Pennsylvania 332 through Newtown to the park.

Washington Crossing State Park

Mileage:	15
Approximate pedaling time:	2 hours
Terrain:	Level, converted railroad bed/canal towpath; mountain bike or hybrid with wide tires recommended
Traffic:	None
Things to see:	Washington Crossing State Park (New Jersey and Pennsylvania), **Bowman's Tower**, antiques shops in Lambertville, views of the Delaware River, forests
Directions at a glance:	For this easy out-and-back ride, get on the **Delaware & Raritan Canal Towpath**, which passes through the park near the entrance on New Jersey 29, and ride north (upstream). No directions are needed.

It's a story we all learned in school: On Christmas night 1776 General George Washington led the Continental Army across the Delaware River at a little-known ferry crossing 8 miles north of Trenton, New Jersey. After landing in New Jersey, the ragtag army engaged Hessian and British troops in the Battles of Trenton and Princeton.

And won: The Battle of Trenton was the military turning point of the Revolutionary War. And were it not for Washington's surprise attack on Christmas night in 1776, we might still be drinking tea and speaking with British accents!

Today the site where Washington and his troops landed is an 841-acre park commemorating that fateful night in 1776. A visitor center that opened in 1976 offers a historical interpretation of the "Ten Critical Days"—December 24, 1776, through January 3, 1777, a period when the Continental Army crossed the Delaware River to fight the two crucial battles, the first major victories over British forces.

The visitor center also houses the **Swan Collection**, composed of 900 military artifacts from the Revolutionary War era. The collection includes items used by soldiers who fought on both sides in the American War of Independence.

Yet there's more than history to Washington Crossing State Park. A 140-acre natural area contains a mixed hardwoods forest that's typical of the piedmont region. An interpretive center provides visitors with exhibits and displays, as well as a nature trail.

Other features in the park include the **Washington Crossing Open Air Theatre**, which can seat 1,000 spectators for concerts and theatrical performances. Three main picnic areas, a group camping area, fishing, and 13 miles of hiking trails round out the attractions available in the park.

Unless, of course, you brought your bike.

Cyclists visiting Washington Crossing State Park can take advantage of the **Delaware and Raritan Canal Towpath**, which passes through the park. After viewing the sights around Washington Crossing, you can take a leisurely, scenic bike cruise north along the trail to Lambertville, New Jersey, a quaint village across the river from New Hope.

After absorbing a lot of eighteenth-century history in the park, move on to the nineteenth century: One hundred years ago the D&R Canal provided the last link in the inland water route between the Pennsylvania coalfields and the steelmills of New York. Coal was transported in barges pulled by mules.

The canal, alas, shut down in the 1930s. But today hikers, joggers, anglers, and bicyclists all find the old canal and restored towpath a recreational treasure.

One reason is the scenery. All along this stretch of the canal are fine views of Bucks County, Pennsylvania, on the opposite shore. Wildlife flourishes along the banks of the river, which is stocked with trout. It's really no surprise that the D&R is the third most popular rail-trail in the United States.

About 1 mile from the park is Titusville, a sleepy little village with a narrow street along the riverbank lined with unpretentious homes and green lawns. Cut off from the mainland by the old canal feeder, the community is almost an island. Back in the old days, the town was a shipping point for grain and produce.

Next you cross Fiddler's Creek, which drains a green valley of rolling farmlands. At around the 4-mile mark, look across the river to a stone observation tower on **Bowman's Hill**—it's usually just visible through the trees. The tower is really a monument erected by the Commonwealth of Pennsylvania on the site of a lookout tower used by American sentries watching river ferries in 1776.

More history: In the hills overlooking the river, Washington's battered army found refuge from British pursuers in December 1776, after the military disasters of Long Island and Fort Washington. The Brits were unable to pursue the American troops into Pennsylvania, because the Americans had taken all of the boats on this part of the Delaware River. Americans kept watch from an outpost on **Goat Hill** as they prepared for their counterattack on Trenton.

Six miles from the park (you're almost in Lambertville!) is the **Wells Falls** of the Delaware, a set of rapids. Old-time raftsmen guiding timber from the upper river to the cities below considered this the most treacherous point on the route.

Soon you roll into Lambertville, a restored village that's a popular destination with tourists. It's one of five nationally registered historic communities along the D&R.

How about lunch? Today **Lambertville Station** is a restaurant that in an earlier incarnation served as the town's train station. But that's not all this village has to offer visitors: Lambertville is filled with shops and restaurants, some quaint, a few unusual—such as the **Cross Country Ski Outfitter** store, a shop devoted entirely to cross-country ski apparel and equipment. The **Full Moon Cafe** is another popular luncheon spot.

On the left is the bridge over the Delaware to New Hope, Pennsylvania, Lambertville's better-known neighbor, famous for its arts and crafts. To the right is a small shopping district with lots of antiques shops (for example, **Haupts Bridge**: "Fine English and Continental

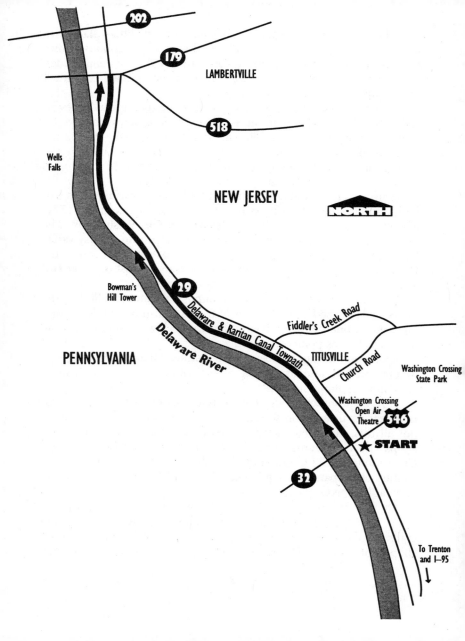

Antiques"), **Rivergate Books,** and several cafes. Now's the time to stop for a bite to eat or to grab a drink!

Dedicated browsers, however, shouldn't miss the **Lambertville Flea Market,** which attracts buyers and sellers from a wide area. It's located across the bridge over the canal.

After a few hours of browsing, shopping, and maybe lunch, it's time to retrace your route back to Bridge Street and pick up the towpath for the return leg to Washington Crossing State Park.

A suggestion: After the ride cross over the bridge to Pennsylvania and visit **Washington Crossing Historic Park,** where General Washington and his men embarked on their historic crossing. In the Memorial Building is a copy of Emanuel Leutze's famous painting, *Washington Crossing the Delaware*—George, by the way, is the one standing. A film showing a reenactment of the event is shown Tuesdays through Sundays.

Then it's back across the Delaware—and you'll have gained a greater appreciation of the ordeal Washington and his troops endured in 1776. Just think, your visit to Washington's Crossing spanned three centuries: the eighteenth and the Revolutionary War, the nineteenth on the D&R Canal, and, finally, the twentieth as you return to your car!

For Further Information

Washington Crossing State Park (609) 737–0623
Visitor Center (609) 737–9304

Getting There

Take I–95 to Yardley Interchange and New Jersey 532, across the river. Park along the Delaware River just past the Approximate Site of the Crossing.

Bulls Island to Frenchtown

Mileage:	16 (8 miles one way)
Approximate pedaling time:	2 hours
Terrain:	Flat
Traffic:	None
Things to see:	Splendid river views, mixed hard-woods forests, the delightful restored village of Frenchtown
Directions at a glance:	No directions are needed for this out-and-back ride along the towpath.

Less than an hour's drive from hectic center-city Philadelphia lies a cyclist's paradise: the Delaware & Raritan Canal State Park. The narrow yet long park is a ribbon of open space that follows the old D&R Canal and the stately Delaware River as they pass through beautiful mixed hardwoods forests on their way to the piedmont hills.

With more than 50 miles of towpath and abandoned railroad beds, the state park offers bicyclists flat, scenic, and traffic-free riding through lush countryside. Here's the best bet if you've never cycled the D&R Canal: the 8-mile bike path between Bulls Island and Frenchtown, one of the most scenic stretches in this New Jersey state park.

Start the ride at **Bulls Island Recreation Center,** an eighty-acre island in the Delaware River featuring picnic sites, hiking and nature trails, a playground, and fishing and boating. For campers there's a seventy-five-site, wooded campground open year-round that offers hot showers and flush toilets—and it's right on the banks of the river!

The bicycle trail, which passes through the campground and is easy to find, leads north to the quaint village of Frenchtown on a converted railroad bed that was once a line of the Pennsylvania Railroad. The right-of-way was turned over to the state in the 1930s and incorporated into the D&R Canal State Park in 1974. This well-maintained rails-to-trails conversion will one day be a link in a developing system of trails extending from Boston to Washington, D.C.

While today the D&R Canal State Park is a bucolic oasis—the noise of traffic on nearby New Jersey 29 is muffled by a band of trees—the canal had a profound effect on the economic development of Pennsylvania and central New Jersey in the nineteenth century.

Opened to barge traffic in 1834, the canal provided a badly needed link connecting the Pennsylvania coalfields and the hungry blast furnaces of New York. The ocean route between Philadelphia and New York was treacherous and long, and the 44-mile canal, which connected the Delaware and Raritan rivers at their heads of navigation, proved to be one of the nation's most efficient—and for decades, busiest—canals.

But the canal era faded with the century as faster, cheaper railroads began to dominate the nation's transportation system. After 1892 the expensive-to-maintain D&R Canal never showed a profit. Forty years later, following the winter of 1932–33, the canal was closed forever.

Yet the D&R Canal's role as a provider of services to the community was far from over. The state of New Jersey restored the feeder canal and the stretch from Trenton and New Brunswick, which became a source of water for farms, industry, and local residents.

The old canal also began providing a new function for the growing towns and cities of New Jersey and Pennsylvania: a wilderness escape. The area along the canal became an informal recreation area as hikers, canoeists, and other outdoors people visited in increasing numbers. In 1974 the 60-mile network of river, canal, and forest was established as a state park.

The campground at Bulls Island makes a wonderful—and convenient—starting point to explore the northern end of the park. Fall is probably the best time of year to combine camping and cycling on the D&R; for one thing, you'll probably have the entire campground to yourself! (A word of warning to campers and picnickers: Keep a sharp eye out for the flock of tame geese that will try to share your feast!) For cyclists the nicest aspect of camping at Bulls Island is the fun of climbing aboard your bike and riding directly from your campsite for a day-long adventure.

The trail heads north from Bulls Island along the Delaware River for approximately 8 miles to Frenchtown. This is *very* easy riding— the trail is wide, flat, and smooth. While a fat-tired mountain or city bike is more stable (the path is unpaved and muddy after a rain), in dry weather your trusty old ten-speed bike works just as well.

In the fall large trees lining the trail form a canopy of blazing orange and crimson overhead. To the left the wide and shallow Delaware River tumbles southward in its journey to the Delaware Bay and the Atlantic Ocean. The biggest challenge to riding the trail is finding a comfortable pace. Relax, take your time, and enjoy the two-hour ride to Frenchtown.

This stretch of bicycle path is great for a family ride: No motorized vehicles are allowed on the trail, and the only people you'll meet as you meander along the river are fellow trail users, such as hikers, joggers, and cyclists. Since it's not widely known that this part of the trail is open for bicycling, it is rarely crowded.

On a quiet morning, especially midweek, most visitors on the trail are treated to a feeling of solitude that's unusual this close to a major city. The river passes through a nearly forgotten part of rural New Jersey and Pennsylvania.

As a result, the park is home to a wide variety of wildlife. Aside from hosting bass, shad, catfish, and trout, the Delaware River is along a principal migratory route for birds. The wooded banks team with wildfowl, since the wild habitat provides favorable nesting sites for migrating birds as they travel the East Coast in the spring and fall. Pack a bird book and look for bobolinks, mockingbirds, and the summer tanager. In the fall you'll see and hear geese and ducks.

People, of course, have made their impact on this stretch of the Delaware River. Most visitors can sense the history—and human suffering—that went into the making of the D&R Canal and the abandoned railroad bed, now a bike path, that continues upriver. As you ride the towpath, think of the thousands of workers, most of them

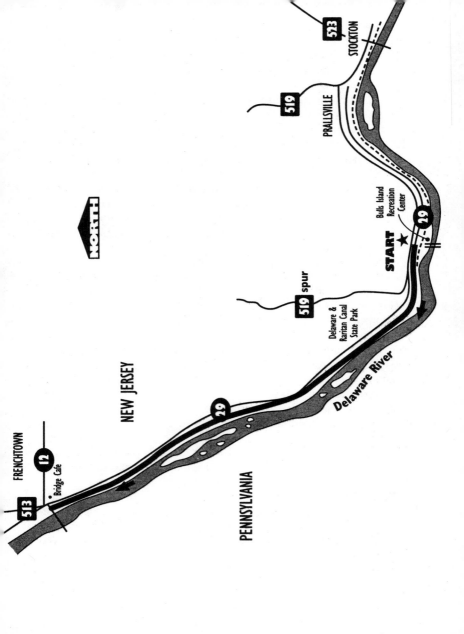

Irish immigrants, who labored for three years to dig the canal. Many of them died in 1832, when cholera swept the labor camps.

But listen more closely: On a summer's morning when a mist hangs on the river, you may hear voices more ancient. It's easy to imagine the Unami Indians, known to the colonial settlers as the Delawares, pursuing their peaceful, riverside existence. A friendly people, the Unamis considered themselves as one with the tribes living on the western bank of the river (now Pennsylvania). Why? Because their neighbors "drank the same water."

The Unamis, part of the Algonkian nation, cooperated with the early white settlers. Later the Sioux referred to the Unamis as "women" because of their peaceful nature—not a sexist sneer but an acknowledgment that it was the tribe's women who could sue for peace.

While the near-wilderness setting of the wooded river valley evokes the memory of the Indians the river is named for, modern amenities occasionally—and thankfully—intrude. Huge stone picnic tables situated at convenient locations along the trail make excellent places to pull over, enjoy a snack, or a take swig out of the water bottle. Often large oak trees loom overhead, offering shelter from the sun on a warm day.

One worry you won't have on this ride is making a wrong turn and getting lost. While the canal ends about 1 mile above Bulls Island, the bike trail continues along the Delaware River. To stay oriented, keep the river to your left as you ride upstream. And if you get tired? On this gentle ride you can turn back at any time and retrace your route to Bulls Island. But Frenchtown shouldn't be missed—it makes the 16-mile round-trip even more worthwhile.

Parlez-vous français?

Don't worry—you won't have any language problems after you roll into Frenchtown.

You'll know you've arrived at this quaint village when you see the gaily striped awnings of the **Bridge Cafe**, the perfect place to stop for lunch or a late-afternoon snack on your Delaware River trek. This bistro is right beside the trail, and you can rest your bike along the fence while stopping for refreshment.

The staff is friendly and the menu is a real treat, featuring large fresh rolls, chocolate chip cookies as large as a plate, and great coffee, as well as traditional fare for heartier appetites. Savor the enchantment of Frenchtown on the Bridge Cafe's outdoor terrace. You can enjoy the weather, take in the lovely river view, and keep an eye on your bike at the same time.

When you're ready to continue your cycling tour, turn right at the bridge and head into this small, irresistible village. You'll pass the **Old Huntingdon House**, a Civil War–era mansion that's now a bed and breakfast. It's easily the largest house in town, and it's set back from the street behind a low wrought-iron fence.

Continue east on Bridge Street (toward the yellow flashing light at the end of town) and you'll come to a charming, brick-paved cul-de-sac. The tiny eighteenth-century houses have been refurbished and glow in the afternoon sun. Windowboxes and pots full of flowers everywhere brighten the facades of the restored residences and lend a European flair to the village.

Frenchtown, with all the charm conjured by its name, is worth spending a few hours exploring. You might browse at **French Country Pottery**—and risk the temptation of splurging on some of the beautiful hand-thrown pottery on display. Check out the antiques shops and the **Race Street Cafe**—a restaurant with a four-star reputation that boasts a popular Sunday brunch. Another stop you'll want to make is **Ron Kobli's Decoys & Wildlife Gallery**. Frenchtown has a lot to offer cyclists—which explains the crowds of two-wheelers that converge here on weekends.

When you're ready to head back—the proprietors of the shops will be glad to hold your purchases or ship them home for you later—simply ride your bike back toward the bridge, turn left onto the trail, and return to Bulls Island on the same path that brought you to Frenchtown.

A pleasant surprise awaits your tired legs—it turns out that the ride north to Frenchtown wasn't really flat but was in fact a very gentle uphill grade. Guess what? The ride back to Bulls Island from the quaint little village on the banks of the Delaware is downhill all the way!

For Further Information

Paul Stern, Superintendent, D&R Canal State Park (201) 397–2949

Getting There

From Philadelphia drive north to New Hope, cross the Delaware River into New Jersey, turn left on to New Jersey 29, and follow the signs to Bulls Island Recreation Area, located 3 miles north of Stockton.

Peddler's Village

Mileage:	12
Approximate pedaling time:	1.5 hours
Terrain:	Rolling, with a couple of steep but short climbs
Traffic:	Light, except around Peddler's Village
Things to see:	Shops in Peddler's Village, sumptuous estates in woodsy settings, restored hamlets, beautiful countryside

Quaint. It's an innocent enough sounding word, with a reassuring dictionary definition: having an old-fashioned attractiveness or charm.

In Bucks County, Pennsylvania, however, quaint is a lot more than just charm—it's an industry. And no wonder: With a landscape awash in pretty woods and fields, picturesque villages, well-manicured lawns surrounding sumptuous stone houses, and narrow, tree-lined lanes, it all adds up to an atmosphere that's the epitome of old-fashioned charm.

Yet Peddler's Village, one of many attractions on this easy spin through Bucks County, manages to take quaintness a step beyond the usual meaning of the word. In a county full of the real thing, it's a re-creation of an eighteenth-century village full of shops and restaurants where tourists walk along winding brick pathways . . . and shop.

But as you would expect in well-heeled Bucks County, the shopping at Peddler's Village is definitely upscale. Merchandise from all over the world—such as exotic furniture, handcrafted chandeliers, handwoven wicker, and homespun fabrics—can be found here.

And more: handmade candies, a Christmas shop, an herb store, handicrafts, sportswear, Scandinavian gifts, quilts, designer handbags,

43

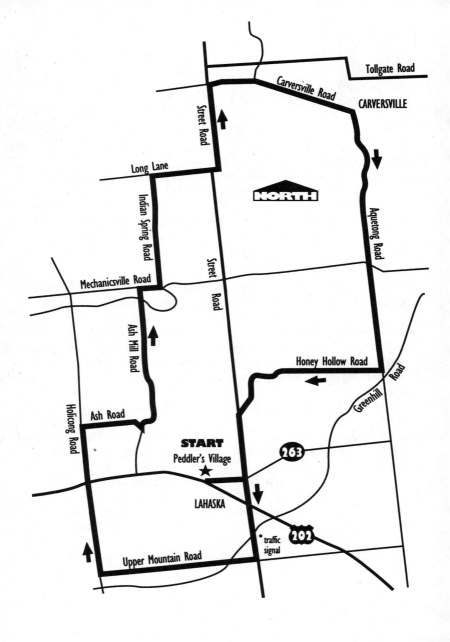

DIRECTIONS at a glance

0.0 Park at Peddler's Village. On your bike head toward Street Road, going south across U.S. 202.

0.2 Go straight at the traffic signal and U.S. 202.

0.66 Turn right onto Upper Mountain Road.

1.87 Turn right onto Holicong Road.

2.6 Go straight at the traffic signal.

3.13 Turn right onto Ash Road.

3.59 Turn left onto Ash Mill Road.

4.73 Turn right onto Mechanicsville Road at the stop sign.

4.9 Turn left onto Indian Springs Road.

5.8 Turn right onto Long Lane.

6.27 Turn left onto Street Road (bear left at the Y; there's a short, steep climb).

6.95 Turn right onto Carversville Road at the stop sign.

8.05 Arrive at Carversville. When leaving the village, turn right onto Aquetong Road, which is followed by a short climb. At the stop sign continue straight on Aquetong Road.

10.25 Turn right onto Honey Hollow Road.

11.59 Turn left onto Street Road.

12.12 Arrive back at Peddler's Village in Lahaska.

---

decorative hardware, heirloom lace, sexy lingerie, leathergoods, international coffees, fresh-roasted nuts, a bath boutique, costume jewelry . . .

Did you bring a credit card?

Nor does Peddler's Village scrimp in the food department. And that's especially good news for people on bicycles on an easy tour of Bucks County.

Hungry? You can choose from classic country dining at **Jenny's Restaurant** (featuring entrees like Mushrooms Pennsylvania and Strawberry-Chicken Bibb Salad), the **Spotted Hog** ("a country bistro and sports bar"), the **Peddler's Pub** (an "Old English" tavern), and, for those in a rush, **Punch 'n Judy**, a hot dog stand.

Aside from the overt commercialism of Peddler's Village, however, there is charm aplenty on this easy ride: winding country lanes; a huge, restored stone house and barns; custom-designed contemporary houses on sumptuous lots.

After starting the ride in Peddler's Village, cyclists cross U.S. 202 and plunge into beautiful countryside. Keep your eyes peeled for some genuine rustic charm on this Bucks County ramble. The delightful village of Carversville, at the bottom of a long downhill run, features the restored Carversville Inn, a fiber studio surrounded by pots of flowers, a general store ("sundries, food, and antiques"), and a cabinet shop.

Like we said, quaint.

A short spin beyond Carversville and you're back on gently rolling roads. (Watch out for a spur from the right just before the stop sign at Mechanicsville Road—traffic moves fast.) Next: more gorgeous homes in woodsy settings. In Lahaska, Peddler's Village is to the right.

One rhetorical question: Is too much quaintness a bad thing? Try this pretty ride and find out for yourself!

For Further Information

Bucks County Tourist Commission (215) 345–4552
Peddler's Village (215) 794–4000

Getting There

From Doylestown go east on U.S. 202 toward Lahaska. Just past the Buckingham Friends School and Meetinghouse, the road splits. Take the left prong of the Y, Route 263. There's plenty of parking around the perimeter of Peddler's Village.

Wycombe Loop

Mileage:	9
Approximate pedaling time:	1 hour
Terrain:	Rolling, with one short, steep climb
Traffic:	Light, except for a short stretch on Durham Road (Pennsylvania 413)
Things to see:	The quaint Pineville Tavern (circa 1742), the Wycombe Inn, beautiful views of gently rolling countryside, pretty country lanes and farms

If there's one word that best describes this short, scenic ride in central Bucks County, it's *tranquil*. The route takes cyclists through a section of the county that has managed to retain its rural flavor despite the encroaching suburban sprawl moving up from the south. As you spin your cranks along the way, you'll see that agriculture still plays a large role in the county's economy. As a result, lots of old farmhouses, barns, and working farms, together with an absence of suburban housing tracts, make this a great cycling destination.

Sights along this pleasant ride include the **White Hall Inn**, a 1794 manorhouse that's been converted into a bed and breakfast. The **Pineville Tavern**, built in 1742, features wide plank floors, 1.5-foot-thick walls, a large bar, two TVs, country music on the jukebox, and Rolling Rock on tap. The tavern is a great lunch stop along the ride. The **Wycombe Inn**, where the ride starts, is a country inn with seven suites and an English pub atmosphere.

The ride begins in the tiny town of Wycombe, a cluster of old homes on Forest Grove Road. Soon you enter an open area of farms where you can see for miles to the wooded ridge line in the distance.

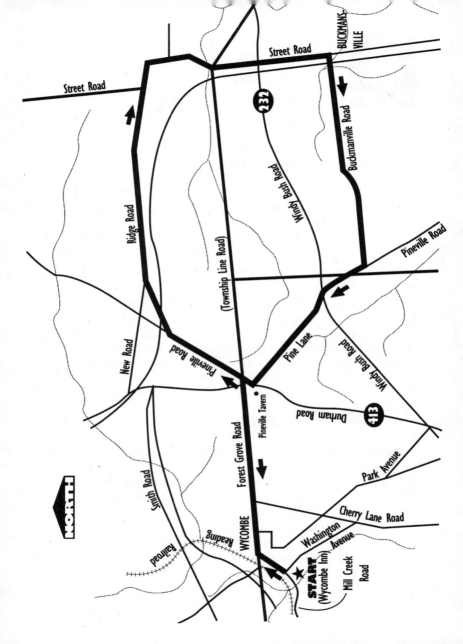

DIRECTIONS
at a glance

0.0	From the Wycombe Inn in Wycombe, turn left onto Mill Creek Road.
0.1	Turn right onto Forest Grove Road in Wycombe.
1.1	Turn left onto Pineville Road (cross Durham Road).
1.6	Turn right onto Ridge Road.

3.3 Continue straight as Ridge Road merges into Street Road.
4.7 Turn right onto Buckmanville Road.
6.1 Turn right onto Pineville Road.
6.4 Cross Windy Bush Road; bear left onto Pine Lane.
7.2 Turn right onto Durham Road (Pennsylvania 413).
7.3 Arrive at the Pineville Tavern, on the right.
7.4 Cross Pennsylvania 413 and turn left onto Forest Grove Road (Township Line Road).
8.6 Turn left onto Mill Creek Road.
8.7 Arrive at the Wycombe Inn.

On Street Road you'll encounter a steep—but short—uphill climb. On Buckmanville Road riders are treated to a rolling section of country lane that passes through woods. On Pineville Road the Whitehall Inn, a large white house, sits on twelve rolling acres. It's one of many large manorhouses nearby. Inside, the bed and breakfast boasts a curving walnut staircase, high ceilings, wide pine floors, and deep-silled, wavy glass windows.

Come to think of it, this is a ride that features a little bit of everything—a great country tavern, bucolic views of rolling countryside, lovely lanes, a country inn, and a bed and breakfast. It's a perfect recipe for a tranquil, country ramble by bike.

For Further Information

Bucks County Tourist Commission (215) 345–4552

Getting There

Doylestown, the largest town near the beginning of this ride, is located about 25 miles north of Philadelphia on Pennsylvania 611. From the U.S. 202 bypass on the southeastern edge of Doylestown, turn right onto Swamp Road, which becomes Forest Grove Road. To reach the Wycombe Inn, turn right onto Mill Creek Road and drive 0.1 mile.

Buckingham "D" Ride

Mileage:	8
Approximate pedaling time:	1 hour
Terrain:	Rolling, with a couple of steep but short climbs
Traffic:	Light
Things to see:	Old Stone Forge, beautiful old stone houses, lush Bucks County countryside

When bike clubs plan different cycling routes for their members, they frequently rank the routes for length and difficulty. And for some of us, the system used is all too reminiscent of high school—"A" through "D." Yet for bike clubs the rating system works like this: An "A" ride is the most difficult, often 100 miles or longer and designed for riders who can go at a blistering pace. A "D" ride, on the other hand, is an easy ride used to introduce new members to the sport.

This ride, centering on the rolling countryside between Doylestown and the Delaware River, is a popular "D" ride with local bike clubs. But don't think of that final grade you got in high school algebra: Here "D" isn't for unsatisfactory. Instead, it stands for short, gentle, and scenic.

This is a fun cruise through the heart of Bucks County—no stores, no villages, just lush countryside, grand stone houses, and quiet roads. In fact, this ride best illustrates why Bucks County is such a popular destination for casual bicyclists.

It's an easy ride too, along roads that are well paved and lightly traveled by cars. This makes for great riding in any season, but especially in the fall, when the leaves on the stately trees that line the roads are full of color.

You can also include this ride with a day of shopping and sight-

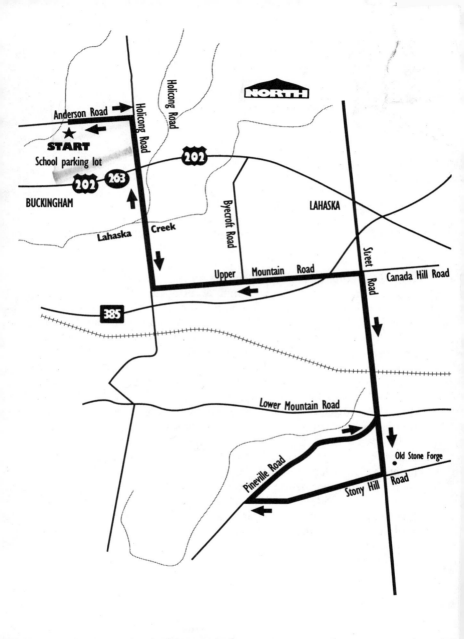

Buckingham "D" Ride

Mileage:	8
Approximate pedaling time:	1 hour
Terrain:	Rolling, with a couple of steep but short climbs
Traffic:	Light
Things to see:	Old Stone Forge, beautiful old stone houses, lush Bucks County countryside

When bike clubs plan different cycling routes for their members, they frequently rank the routes for length and difficulty. And for some of us, the system used is all too reminiscent of high school—"A" through "D." Yet for bike clubs the rating system works like this: An "A" ride is the most difficult, often 100 miles or longer and designed for riders who can go at a blistering pace. A "D" ride, on the other hand, is an easy ride used to introduce new members to the sport.

This ride, centering on the rolling countryside between Doylestown and the Delaware River, is a popular "D" ride with local bike clubs. But don't think of that final grade you got in high school algebra: Here "D" isn't for unsatisfactory. Instead, it stands for short, gentle, and scenic.

This is a fun cruise through the heart of Bucks County—no stores, no villages, just lush countryside, grand stone houses, and quiet roads. In fact, this ride best illustrates why Bucks County is such a popular destination for casual bicyclists.

It's an easy ride too, along roads that are well paved and lightly traveled by cars. This makes for great riding in any season, but especially in the fall, when the leaves on the stately trees that line the roads are full of color.

You can also include this ride with a day of shopping and sight-

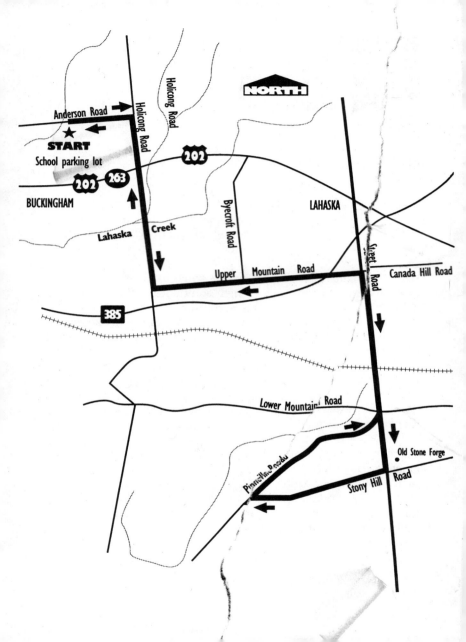

**DIREC-
TIONS
at a glance**

0.0	Turn left out of the school parking lot onto Anderson Road.
0.1	Turn right onto Holicong Road at the stop sign.
0.4	Go straight at the traffic signal and cross U.S. 202 and Pennsylvania 263.
1.13	Turn left onto Upper Mountain Road and pass Byecroft Road on the left.

2.33 Turn right onto Street Road and cross Lower Mountain Road.

3.55 Turn right onto Stony Hill Road.

4.33 Turn right onto Pineville Road at the stop sign (the sign may be hidden by a cedar tree).

5.24 Turn left onto Street Road at the stop sign.

6.11 Turn left onto Upper Mountain Road.

7.32 Turn right onto Holicong Road.

8.05 Go straight across U.S. 202 and Pennsylvania 263 at the traffic signal.

8.35 Turn left onto Anderson Road.

8.45 Turn right into the school parking lot.

seeing in nearby New Hope or at the **Mercer Museum** and the **Moravian Pottery and Tile Works** in Doylestown. Or consider this popular option: Spend the weekend at one of the many bed and breakfasts in Bucks County, and use this ride for an afternoon or morning spin.

The ride starts at the Anderson School, where you can park in the lot nearest the road. On weekends the lot is usually empty. Yet even on school days, you'll find a space to park in the outer lot. Before pedaling off, stop for a moment to soak up the quiet and the rural feel that envelops you after the hustle and bustle of U.S. 202.

After crossing U.S. 202 and Pennsylvania 263, Holicong Road turns into a narrow country lane bordered by sumptuous, well-kept old houses on magnificent lots. Soon you come to a one-lane bridge with lovely stonework that matches the house on the large estate to your right. Upper Mountain Road is a rolling country lane, with views of the farmlands to the right and left.

After turning onto Street Road and crossing Lower Mountain

Road, gear down for a rather steep but short climb. It's worth the effort, though, to see the **Old Stone Forge** that soon appears on the left. Stop for a few minutes to look at the low stone walls and the ruins of the original dwelling.

Now the real reward for the effort you put into pedaling up that hill: a wonderfully invigorating descent on Stony Hill Road. At the stop sign look for the street sign for Pineville Road—it may be hidden behind a cedar tree. Pineville Road is a woodsy country lane with a couple of short, gradual climbs. Remember that wonderful descent just a couple of miles back? Now you pay the price. Relax—these hills are easy.

You'll recognize Upper Mountain Road again, and Holicong Road, lined with huge oak trees that offer shade during summer. Be careful crossing U.S. 202 and Pennsylvania 263—the intersection can be busy at times.

Soon you're back in the parking lot where the ride started. If this scenic ride whetted your appetite for more riding in Bucks County— and you have the time—pick up a county map and explore more of these lovely roads.

And you'll do it with the knowledge of how bike clubs grade their club rides: When it comes to Bucks County, "D" does *not* mean unsatisfactory!

For Further Information

Bucks County Tourist Commission (215) 345–4552

Getting There

From Doylestown go east on U.S. 202 and turn left on Pennsylvania 413 (Durham Road), then right on Anderson Road. Park in the Anderson School parking lot, on the left.

Doylestown to New Hope Loop

Mileage:	25
Approximate pedaling time:	3 hours
Terrain:	Rolling, with a few short, steep climbs and a long climb out of Carversville
Traffic:	Light, except inside the towns
Things to see:	Moravian Pottery and Tile Works, Fonthill Museum, Mercer Museum, James A. Michener Arts Center (Doylestown); Bucks County Playhouse, New Hope & Ivyland Railroad, New Hope–Parry Barn, Mule Barge, Coryell's Ferry Boat Rides, Boat Rides at Wells Ferry (New Hope); beautiful backcountry roads and farmland

Bucks County! Home of James Michener, Pearl Buck, and other writers and artists, as well as of beautiful countryside, lazy afternoons, romantic bed and breakfasts, antiques shopping . . . the list goes on. There's something for everybody, from history buffs to art collectors to avid shoppers—and, of course, ardent bicyclists. Feel the tensions of city and job drain away as you spin along these lush sylvan roads.

To begin this scenic Bucks County ramble that loops from Doylestown through the art village of New Hope and back, drive to the starting point along Pennsylvania 313. To your right look for a structure that resembles a medieval monastery—it's the **Moravian Pottery and Tile Works**, where the ride begins. The museum is operated by the Bucks County Parks and Recreation Commission and is handy for folks exploring the county by bike. You'll find ample parking, water, and restrooms.

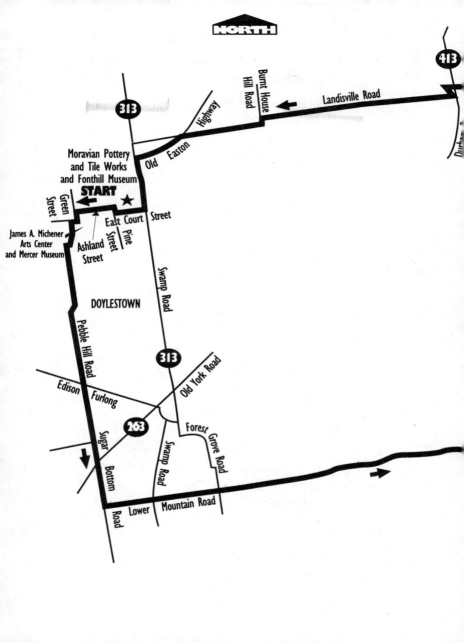

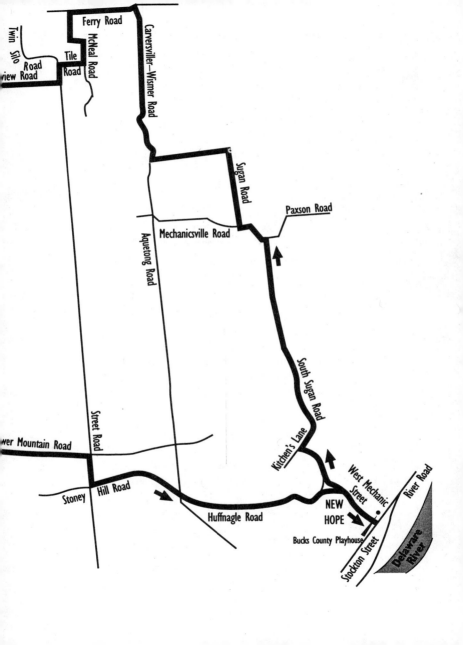

**DIREC-
TIONS
at a glance**

0.0 Leave the Fonthill Museum parking lot and turn right onto East Court Street.
0.7 Turn left onto Pine Street; cross Oakland Street.
0.9 Turn left onto Ashland Street.
1.0 Turn left onto Green Street, which becomes Pebble Hill Road and then Sugar Bottom Road.
4.1 Cross Old York Road (Pennsylvania 263).
4.3 Bear left onto Lower Mountain Road (a cutoff leading to the main road).
4.6 Turn left onto Lower Mountain Road.
9.8 Turn right onto Street Road.
10.1 Turn left onto Stoney Hill Road (the name changes to Huffnagle Road); at the mill go straight.
13.1 Turn right onto West Mechanic Street in New Hope.
13.7 Turn left onto Stockton Street.

Leaving New Hope

13.7 Turn right onto West Mechanic Street.
14.2 Turn right at the Y onto South Sugan Road.
15.5 Turn right at the intersection (to stay on Sugan Road).
19.6 Turn left onto Paxson Road.
23.9 Turn left onto Mechanicsville Road (the sign, however, says Cuttalossa Road).
24.0 Turn right onto Sugan Road.
25.0 Turn left onto Saw Mill Road.
26.0 Turn left onto Aquetong Road.
26.6 Turn left onto Carversville Road; make an immediate right after the bridge onto Wismer Road.
28.1 Turn left onto Ferry Road.
28.9 Turn left onto McNeal Road.
29.7 Turn right onto Twin Silo Road.
30.0 Turn left onto Ridgeview Road.
31.4 Turn left onto Durham Road (Pennsylvania 413).

31.5	Turn right onto Landisville Road.
32.9	Turn left at Burnt House Hill Road, then make an immediate right to continue on Landisville Road.
33.9	Bear left onto Old Easton Highway.
34.7	Turn left onto Swamp Road (Pennsylvania 313).
35.1	Turn right into the Moravian Pottery and Tile Works parking lot.

It's a site worth exploring before or after your ride. This National Historic Landmark functions as a living history museum. Founded by Henry Mercer earlier in the century, the operation still produces tiles using original methods. The museum offers self-guided tours every half-hour—and don't miss the museum shop. Hours are 10:00 A.M. to 5:00 P.M. daily.

Mercer, a leader in the arts-and-crafts movement, lived in today's **Fonthill Museum**, located at the end of the drive toward East Court Street. The castlelike building features tours of more than forty different rooms. Built to exhibit Mercer's collection of prints and tiles from around the world, the mansion includes Mercer's Library, the Saloon, and the Columbus Room.

Doylestown is the county seat of Bucks County but retains a small-town flavor. After cycling through the shady lanes on the start of this ride, you'll come to the **Mercer Museum**, founded by—you guessed it—Henry Mercer. His first exhibition, "The Tools of the Nation Maker," was shown in 1897. The museum was built to house his collection of tools and implements, and these provide a glimpse into the daily lives and tasks of eighteenth- and nineteenth-century Americans.

Across Pine Street is the **James A. Michener Arts Center**, formerly the Bucks County jail. A section of the former prison yard is now home to a sculpture garden, and the main exhibition gallery fills the remainder. Named after the world-famous author and Bucks County native, the reconstructed building promotes the arts through its collection of twentieth-century American art and ongoing cultural programs.

As you turn onto Green Street, you'll be leaving "downtown" Doylestown. You'll ride on a wide shoulder, and you'll blast down a

big downhill. As you travel through this easy, rolling terrain, your eyes are drawn to beautiful stone houses with well-manicured lawns and ponds populated with ducks and geese. It's suburbia, Bucks County style. Soon, however, you're in the country spinning past lovely pastures and farmfields on nearly traffic-free roads. In the autumn ripening gourds and pumpkins add splashes of color to the countryside.

Alas, traffic increases as you approach New Hope, a village on the Delaware River famous for its arts and crafts. Turn left on Stockton to begin your exploration of this quaint, riverside community. It's best to either park your bike (bring a lock) or walk it, since the main street, Pennsylvania 32, lacks a shoulder. And watch out for pedestrians: New Hope, a popular destination for tourists, is usually crowded with foot traffic.

New Hope has long been muse to the artistic spirit. There's the **Bucks County Playhouse**, a favorite of celebrities during the summer season. Galleries featuring antiques, paintings, pottery, wearable art, jewelry, and exotic collections abound throughout New Hope. There's lots to see and do here.

Tired of shopping and sightseeing? Stop in at **Gerenser's Exotic Ice Cream** ("Desserts from sensible to sinful!") on South Main Street for a pick-me-up. For lunch there's no shortage of restaurants and cafes to choose from in New Hope.

After a meal consider a river excursion: **Coryell's Ferry Boat Rides** offers half-hour cruises on the Delaware and one- to three-hour charters. Another option is the **Mule Barge**, a ride on a mule-drawn barge through the **Delaware Canal**, a state park and National Historic Landmark. It's one of only a few preserved canals in the United States. Tours are available from April through November 15.

Another option: a trip on the **New Hope & Ivyland Rail Road**, which runs an old-fashioned steam train through the Bucks County countryside to Lahaska. You'll learn history and legend as you pass the sights on this 9-mile, fifty-minute trip.

By now you should be ready to continue the loop back to Doylestown. Retrace your route back to Mechanic Street and get ready for some uphill riding: You're riding away from the river, so you'll be doing some climbing. At the Y bear right across the railroad tracks to Sugan Road. Soon you're spinning past beautiful stuccoed houses in the country as you complete this loop through Bucks County.

Here's another option for two-wheel tourists who would like to combine a bike tour with a romantic stay at an upscale inn: Spend a night or two at one of the many bed and breakfasts in New Hope. You can ride the same route starting in New Hope, explore Doylestown, and then ride back to your inn. Call the Bucks County Tourist Commission for a list of bed and breakfasts in New Hope.

For Further Information

Bucks County Tourist Commission (215) 345–4552
Historic New Hope (215) 862–5880

Getting There

From the Pennsylvania Turnpike's Willow Grove exit, go north on U.S. 611. Take the U.S. 611 bypass around Doylestown to the Pennsylvania 313 exit (Swamp Road). Turn right, continue a short distance to the Moravian Pottery and Tile Works on the right, and park.

Valley Forge

Mileage:	6.5
Approximate pedaling time:	1 hour
Terrain:	Rolling, with a couple of hills
Traffic:	None
Things to see:	Reconstructed log huts, military re-doubts, eighteenth-century stone farmhouses, monuments, beautifully manicured parklands
Directions at a glance:	The bike trail, which starts at the visitor center, is well marked and easy to follow.

It takes only a few simple words to convey the meaning of Valley Forge to Americans: *suffering, sacrifice, triumph*. While no bayonet charges or artillery barrages shattered the stillness around Valley Forge during the winter of 1777–78, this encampment on the Schuylkill River best symbolizes the struggle that was the American Revolution.

Some background: In the late summer of 1777, Sir William Howe, commander of British forces in North America, landed an experienced army at the upper end of Chesapeake Bay. His objective was to march north and capture Philadelphia, the Patriot capital. To defend the city General George Washington maneuvered his army into position, but the troops lost the Battle of Brandywine and fought to a draw at Germantown. The British occupied Philadelphia.

With cold weather setting in, Washington sought winter quarters for his decimated army. He chose Valley Forge, 18 miles northwest of Philadelphia, for several reasons: It was close enough to the capital to keep British forces from raiding interior Pennsylvania but was far

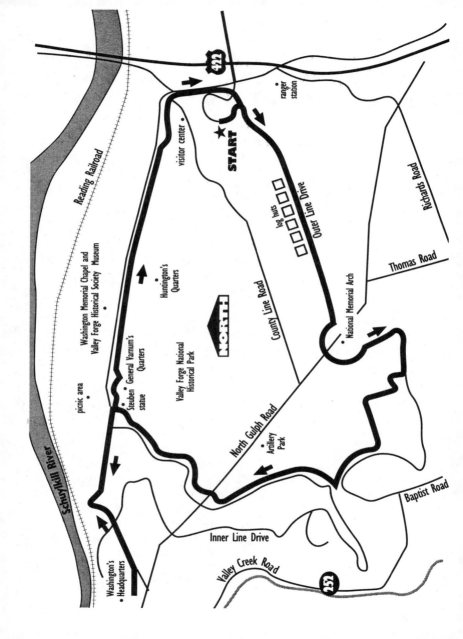

enough away to discourage a surprise British attack. Further, the high ground around Valley Forge made it easily defensible.

Conditions that winter were severe, and the 12,000 men of the Grand Army suffered. Supplies such as food, blankets, and clothing were inadequate, and disease swept the camp. As many as 2,000 men died that winter.

Yet during the terrible six months that Washington's army remained encamped at Valley Forge, a new fighting force was created. Friedrich von Steuben, a former member of the elite general staff of Frederick the Great of Prussia, volunteered his military skills to the Patriot cause. He set up an effective training program that transformed the ragtag army into a real fighting force. It emerged in June 1778 to pursue Howe's forces into New Jersey as they marched on New York.

Today Valley Forge is an oasis of green fields and woods surrounded by superhighways, high-rises, and suburban sprawl. Cyclists, joggers, and tourists flock to the beautiful park year-round. A 6-mile paved bicycle path allows visitors on bikes to tour the park at a leisurely pace.

Touring Valley Forge by bike also imparts a feel for the terrain as you pedal up and down the rolling hills. Along the way you'll pass reconstructed log huts where General Peter Muhlenberg's brigade anchored the outer line of defense. The imposing **National Arch** was dedicated in 1917 to commemorate the "patience and fidelity" of the soldiers who wintered here.

Farther along on the tour, you pass **Artillery Park**, where most of the cannons brought to Valley Forge were massed. In case of an attack, the cannons could be dispatched from this central position to wherever they were needed. **General Varnum's Quarters** is an early-eighteenth-century farmhouse overlooking the parade grounds. Nearby is a statue of General von Steuben, who led the training of the army during that winter. Close at hand is a picnic area (with restrooms) where you can stop and enjoy a brown-bag lunch.

An out-and-back spur of the bike trail leads to **Washington's Headquarters**, a stone house that the army's commander sublet from widow Deborah Hewes. Originally Washington promised his suffer-

ing troops that, like them, he would live in a tent. But a heavy snow-fall on Christmas Day forced a change of mind. The area also features reconstructed huts that housed the commander-in-chief's guards.

On the final stretch of the bike route, look for the **Washington Memorial Chapel** and **Valley Forge Historical Society Museum**, lo-cated on private property within the park. The museum contains arti-facts from the Revolutionary War.

A long downhill run and a short climb return you to the visitor center—and restrooms and water. As you load your bike on your car, think about the sites you just saw: From your self-propelled tour of Valley Forge and its huts, memorials, monuments, and markers, you will have learned the story of the men who wrote one of the greatest chapters in American history.

For Further Information

Valley Forge National Park Visitor Center (215) 783–1077

Getting There

Valley Forge is located 18 miles northwest of Philadelphia at the in-tersection of the Pennsylvania Turnpike (I–76) and U.S. 422. Follow signs to the park entrance, and park in the lot located past the visitor center.

Phoenixville Loop

Mileage:	28
Approximate pedaling time:	3 hours
Terrain:	Rolling, with a couple of short but steep climbs
Traffic:	Light, except in Phoenixville and for short stretches along Pennsylvania 29, Pothouse Road, and Pennsylvania 113
Things to see:	Three covered bridges; fast-moving French, Pine, and Pickering creeks; a winery; tiny backroads and beautiful rural countryside

The suburban enclave of Phoenixville, located about 25 miles west of Philadelphia (a few miles northwest of Valley Forge), looks just like any other small town in crowded Chester County. But only a few miles outside its limits, the suburban sprawl drops away and intrepid cycle tourists are plunged into a breathtaking panorama of rural beauty, fast-flowing streams, quaint covered bridges, forests, sumptuous estates, and twisting, nearly traffic-free backcountry roads. It's one heck of a bike ride.

The route begins in Phoenixville on Starr Street, which intersects with Pennsylvania 23 in the center of town. Park in the lot of the grocery store, and ride your bike to the right on Starr Street as you exit the parking lot. A quick left sets you up to cross busy Pennsylvania 23, and soon you're spinning away into the rolling Pennsylvania countryside.

Three miles later, **Rapps Bridge**, the first of three covered bridges on the ride, comes into view. On the left is **Snyders Mill**, an eighteenth-

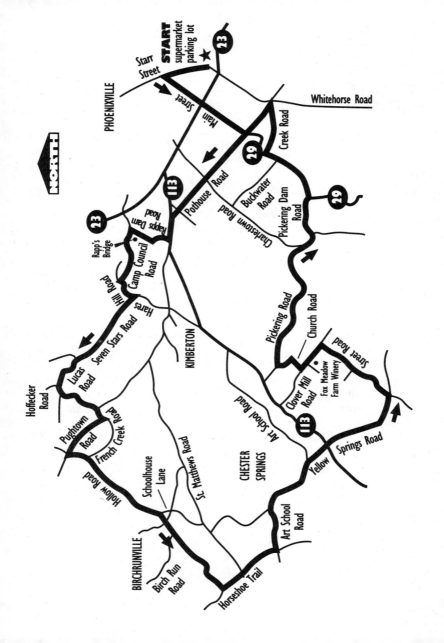

DIREC-TIONS at a glance

0.0	Turn right out of the supermarket parking lot on Starr Street near its intersection with Pennsylvania 23 in downtown Phoenixville.
0.2	Turn left onto Pennsylvania 29 (Main Street).
0.4	Go straight across Pennsylvania 23.
1.3	Turn right onto Pothouse Road.
2.3	Go straight across Charlestown Road.
3.0	Turn left onto Pennsylvania 113.
3.5	Turn right onto Rapps Dam Road.
4.1	Ride through the covered bridge and immediately turn left onto Camp Council Road.
5.0	Turn left onto Hares Hill Road.
5.4	Turn right onto Seven Stars Road.
5.7	Ride straight through the covered bridge.
6.7	Turn left onto Lucas Road.
7.4	Turn left onto Hoffecker Road.
7.6	Cross the bridge over the creek.
8.0	Turn right onto Pughtown Road.
8.2	Ride through the covered bridge over the creek.
9.0	Turn left onto Hollow Road.
11.1	Go straight past Birch Run Road.
12.3	Turn left onto Horseshoe Trail.
13.3	Turn left onto Art School Road.
14.9	Turn right onto Yellow Springs Road.
15.3	Go straight across Pennsylvania 113.
16.8	Turn left onto Street Road.
18.1	Turn left onto Clover Mill Road.
19.0	Pass Fox Meadow Farm Winery.
19.4	Turn right onto Church Road.
19.8	Turn right onto Pickering Road.
20.9	Turn left onto Merlin Road (detour on Pickering).
21.2	Turn right onto Lincoln Road (detour on Pickering).
21.9	Turn left onto Pickering Road.
22.7	Turn right onto Charlestown Road.
23.1	Turn left onto Pickering Dam Road.

23.9	Bear left onto Pennsylvania 29.
24.7	Turn right onto Creek Road.
25.7	Turn left onto Whitehorse Road, then immediately turn left onto Pothouse Road.
26.4	Turn right onto State Road (Pennsylvania 29; the name changes to Main Street).
27.2	Go straight across Pennsylvania 23.
27.5	Turn right onto Starr Street.
27.7	Turn left into the supermarket parking lot.

century mill under renovation. The next few miles of rolling lanes take cyclists through lush suburbs and open fields. Another covered bridge comes into sight on Seven Stars Road, followed by more roller-coaster riding along a fast-flowing creek.

Pughtown Road takes you to the last covered bridge on the route; it's in a beautiful, wooded setting that feels like wilderness. More riding along Hollow Road and Horseshoe Trail takes cyclists along a wooded part of Pennsylvania backcountry that suggests the placid backroads of Vermont. Soon Art School Road leads you to Seven Springs Road and single-lane bridges across meandering creeks. A long climb finishes at Street Road, where you turn left.

Street Road may have a redundant name, but it's a spectacular, rollicking road that energetic cyclists will love. It plunges up and over a long ridge that offers terrific views of the surrounding countryside. The final climb on the approach to Clover Mill Road is steep but short.

The countryside, it seems, just keeps getting better the farther along you get on this ride: Pickering Road is a one-lane road that follows a fast-moving creek through beautiful woods. Pickering Dam Road also features a remote, almost wilderness ambience. Finally, you make a right onto Creek Road and begin to approach Phoenixville and the end of the ride.

While this blast of a ride is great for strong riders on lightweight road bikes, folks riding fat-tired mountain or city bikes will appreciate the greater stability those bikes provide as you cycle along these narrow lanes. Some of the road surfaces, especially along the creeks, are pretty beat up, and fat tires pumped up to around 70 psi really smooth out the bumps.

For Further Information

Chester County Tourist Bureau (800) 228–9933.

Getting There

Phoenixville is located on Pennsylvania 23 about 3 miles northwest of Valley Forge, which is on I–76 about 20 miles northwest of downtown Philadelphia.

Hibernia County Park

Mileage:	6 miles unpaved and 2.5 miles paved
Approximate pedaling time:	1 to 3 hours
Terrain:	Rolling
Traffic:	Very light on paved roads; nonexistent on unpaved trails
Things to see:	Hibernia Mansion, meadows, woodlands, Brandywine Creek
Directions at a glance:	No directions are needed to ride the roads and trails in the park. Stop at the office to pick up a free map and to check trail conditions before you ride.

Recently there's been a revolution in cycling: the mountain bike. Equipped with upright handlebars, beefy brakes, easy-to-shift gears, and fat tires, this new breed of bicycle has taken America by storm. Today mountain bikes account for nearly two-thirds of all new bike sales.

Why the sudden popularity of the new style of bike? A trio of reasons. First, people like the solid, secure feel they get when they ride the bikes. Second, to most folks the upright bars feel more comfortable when compared with the drop handlebars on racing bikes. And last but not least, rugged mountain bikes are ideal for riding off-road, whether on dirt roads, paved river paths, or trails.

In other words, people have discovered that riding a bike in the woods is, well, fun. It's like being a kid all over again. They've also figured out something else that has no small appeal to cyclists who feel crowded out when riding a bike on America's roads: There's no traffic in the woods.

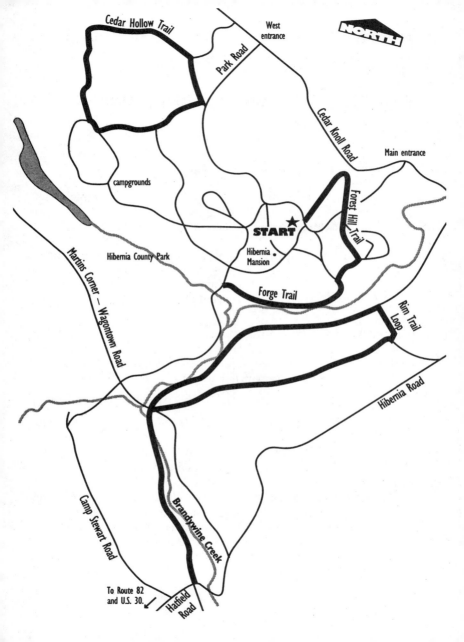

One of the best destinations for folks who own a mountain bike and hate traffic is Hibernia County Park, in western Chester County, Pennsylvania. While it's only a short drive from Philadelphia, the park is located in a wooded setting that quickly makes you forget the city. The 800-acre park includes woodlands and meadows, miles of trails, open fields, and picnic areas. And mountain bikers are welcome to ride it all.

The park boasts 2.5 miles of paved road and 6 miles of multiuse trails ideal for off-road cycling. The trails lead cyclists through forests and fields where you can see wildlife, fish in Brandywine Creek, or stop for a picnic lunch. In addition, Hibernia provides primitive camping facilities with eighteen tent sites and twenty trailer sites.

The grounds also feature **Hibernia Mansion,** the home of an early ironmaster. Seasonal tours are given of the large house and grounds. The entire site is on the National Register of Historic Places.

You can ride as much or as little as you like at this compact park. Cedar Hollow Trail is a 1-mile-long loop located near the group camping area, while the Forest Hill Trail can be ridden in a loop or to connect with the Rim Trail Loop and a ride along Brandywine Creek. All the loops are connected by paved park roads.

The moral: If you've got a fat-tired bike and you're weary of battling for your piece of the pavement, make a beeline for Hibernia County Park.

For Further Information

Hibernia County Park (215) 384–0290

Getting There

The park is located approximately 30 miles west of Philadelphia, 2 miles north on Pennsylvania 82 where it intersects with U.S. 30. Follow signs to the park entrance.

French Creek State Park

Mileage:	32
Approximate pedaling time:	Variable; short loop rides and longer rides lasting several hours are possible on the park's roads and trails
Terrain:	Rolling to steep
Traffic:	None on the trails; light on the roads
Things to see:	Beautiful forests and lakes, a restored early American ironmaking community, wildlife
Directions at a glance:	No directions are required to ride the many trails located inside the park. Pick up a free map at the park office. Since mountain biking is a relatively new sport, trail access is in a state of flux. Check at the office to ensure that all trails are open to cyclists and to get the latest word on trail conditions before you ride.

French Creek State Park, while only 40 miles or so from Philadelphia, is a world away from the hustle and bustle of the big city. With 7,339 acres of forests, meadows, and lakes, the park offers visitors a touch of Appalachia—but it's located within an easy day's drive of town. Mountain bikers who enjoy riding challenging single-track trails will enjoy tackling the miles of hiking paths that permeate the park.

Folks whose interests don't extend to "cleaning" technical trails (that's mountain-biker lingo for riding over something without putting a foot down—or crashing) will still find lots to do at French

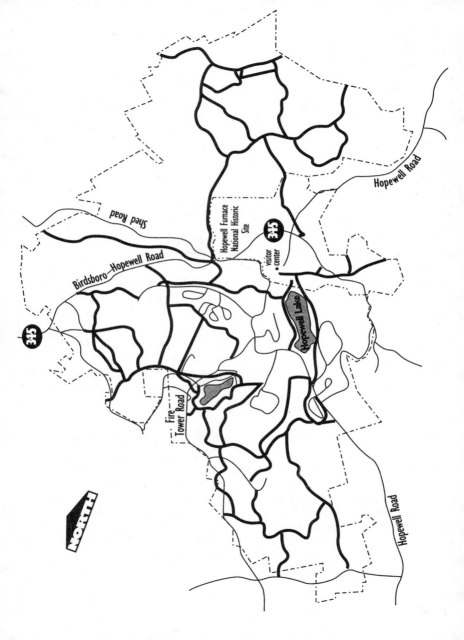

Creek. Miles of paved roads in the park lead to lakes, group campgrounds, a fire tower, and family camping areas. The low gears of a mountain or a hybrid bike will come in handy on the paved roads that go up the steep hills at French Creek.

Yet riding through a beautiful forest while spinning the cranks isn't the only diversion in these lovely hills. Next door to the park is **Hopewell Furnace National Historic Site**, a restored early American ironmaking community. Ore for the furnace was mined locally, and the final product, iron, was used to make firearms carried in the Revolutionary War by American forces. During the summer costumed historical interpreters demonstrate, describe, and tell the story of Hopewell's ironmaking era. Younger children will enjoy seeing the farm animals. To reach this spick-and-span National Park Service–administered site, go out the park entrance to Pennsylvania 345, and turn left.

Other attractions in French Creek include picnicking, swimming in **Hopewell Lake** (from Memorial Day through Labor Day), orienteering with map and compass on the trails, renting a boat on sixty-eight-acre Hopewell Lake, camping, and fishing. You can even rent cabins inside the park.

But just checking out the park's array of flora and fauna is enough for most folks—and it's a great excuse to explore by bike. The park's forest is a combination of northern and southern hardwood trees, giving these woods a wide variety of vegetation, including white flowering dogwood, pink azalea, mountain laurel, sassafras, white pine, hemlock, red maple, and several types of oak.

Among the wildlife living in the park are whitetail deer, red and gray fox, raccoons, gray squirrels, cottontail rabbits, ring-necked pheasants, quail, ruffed grouse, and wild turkeys. Waterfowl found near the lakes include Canada geese, mallards, mergansers, wood ducks, green herons, and, occasionally, blue herons. Nearby fields and forests are home to a myriad of songbirds, as well as to a number of predatory birds, such as great horned owls, screech owls, ospreys, redtail hawks, Cooper's hawks, and American kestrels.

One thing's for sure: For cyclists who enjoy the outdoors, traffic-free riding, and near-wilderness settings, French Creek State Park may be one of the best destinations this side of the Appalachian Mountains.

For Further Information

French Creek State Park (215) 582–1514.

Getting There

French Creek State Park is located about 40 miles west of Philadelphia and 7 miles northeast of the Pennsylvania Turnpike's Morgantown interchange (exit 22) on Pennsylvania 345.

Brandywine Battlefield Loop

Mileage:	16
Approximate pedaling time:	2 hours
Terrain:	Rolling
Traffic:	Light, except along U.S. 1, where there's a wide shoulder
Things to see:	Old stone houses, fences, and barns; horse farms and gorgeous countryside dotted with stunning homes; Longwood Gardens, a former Du Pont estate; a mushroom farm; an art museum; a Revolutionary War battlefield

In 1777 Philadelphia, the new capital of the fledgling United States, was the military objective of British General William Howe, who had landed an experienced army on the shores of the Chesapeake Bay in Maryland and was marching north toward his goal. Standing in his way were General George Washington and a force of American troops determined to hold off the British force.

On September 9 Washington positioned his troops along the Brandywine River to guard the main fords, picking the high ground around Chadds Ford to concentrate his principal force. But the British army, grouped at Kennett Square, split; a portion marched as if to engage Washington at Chadds Ford, while a larger force under Howe marched north and crossed the Brandywine at a ford unknown to the American army. Attacked on the right flank, Washington's army was unable to defend its position and retreated to Chester. Later in the month the British marched into Philadelphia.

Well, maybe it's not the brightest chapter in American history, but

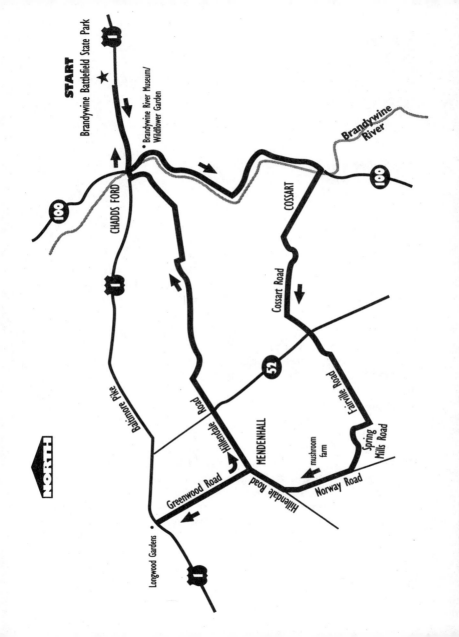

DIREC-TIONS at a glance

0.0   Turn right onto U.S. 1 from Brandywine Battlefield State Park.

0.8   Turn left onto Pennsylvania 100.

2.1   Go straight across the bridge over Brandywine River.

3.0   Turn right onto Cossart Road (the first right after the bridge).

4.8   Turn left onto Fairville Road.

5.1   Go straight at the stop sign.

6.3   Turn right onto Spring Mills Road (no sign).

7.0   Turn right onto Norway Road.

7.6   Go straight past the mushroom farm on the right.

7.7   Go straight across Burrows Run Road (no sign); immediately bear right onto Hillendale Road.

8.2   Turn left onto Greenwood Road.

9.3   Turn right onto the shoulder of U.S. 1; immediately bear right onto the ramp to Longwood Gardens.

9.7   Arrive at Longwood Gardens. After touring the gardens ride toward U.S. 1 past the visitor center.

9.9   Cross U.S. 1, turn left, then immediately turn right onto Greenwood Road and retrace your route.

11.0   Turn left onto Hillendale Road.

14.1   Go straight across the railroad tracks and turn left at the stop sign onto Fairville Road.

15.0   Turn right onto the shoulder of U.S. 1.

15.2   Pass the Brandywine River Museum on the right.

15.3   Go straight past the intersection with Pennsylvania 100.

16.1   Turn left into Brandywine Battlefield State Park.

the valiant lesson from America's past provides a great excuse to take your bike to this beautiful park and ride through some quaint and picturesque countryside. Starting at the fifty-acre park, cyclists can spin along charming lanes that follow the Brandywine River and pass horse farms. At the same time, two-wheeled travelers can marvel at the sumptuous homes—both honest-to-God colonials and magnificent contemporaries—that clutter the landscape.

Either before or after your ride, be sure to check out the Brandywine Battlefield State Park's visitor center, which features a small museum and an audiovisual presentation that makes the battle come alive. Two other sites in the park are **Washington's Headquarters**, a farmhouse where the general planned his strategy, and **Lafayette's Headquarters**, the house where the young French volunteer was quartered on the eve of the battle. A warning: The park is quite hilly, and unless you're already warmed up from riding, it's probably easier to stroll than to ride to the houses. Fat-tire cyclists should stick to the pavement; no off-road riding is permitted on the state park's grounds.

Begin the ride by exiting the park and riding 1 mile south on the wide shoulder of U.S. 1 to Pennsylvania 100, where you turn left. You immediately plunge into eighteenth-century America as you roll along wooded lanes, stone fences and houses, and the meandering Brandywine River. Turn right after the bridge over the river onto Cossart Road, a small lane that winds its way past horse farms and woods. On Fairville Road the countryside gets more suburban, but the riding is delightful and the traffic is light.

After you reach Hillendale Road, turn left onto Greenwood Road for an out-and-back ride to **Longwood Gardens**, 350 acres of exotic flowers, spectacular fountains, and special exhibits. After you return to Hillendale Road, you'll discover it's a delightful roller-coaster romp through rural countryside. Get as much speed as you can on the descents so you can make it up the next hill with a minimum of effort. Soon you're back to U.S. 1. Turn right and follow the shoulder a short distance to the **Brandywine River Museum**, which features art by the Wyeth family and other American artists. Brandywine Battlefield State Park is 1 mile down U.S. 1, on the left.

For Further Information

Brandywine Valley Tourist Information (800) 228–9933

Getting There

Brandywine Battlefield State Park is located about 20 miles southwest of Philadelphia on U.S. 1, south of its intersection with U.S. 202.

Nottingham County Park

Mileage:	8
Approximate pedaling time:	1 to 2 hours
Terrain:	Rolling
Traffic:	None
Things to see:	Woodlands, ponds, outcroppings of serpentine stone, rare and unique plants and birds, a small covered bridge
Directions at a glance:	No directions are required to ride the 8 miles of multiuse trails in the park. Check with the Ranger Office near the park entrance for the latest trail conditions, recommendations on trails to ride, and a free map. Maps are usually available at the kiosk across from the office.

Nottingham County Park is a refuge for casual fat-tired cyclists seeking relief from the pressures and frustrations of sharing the road with cars. The park's 8 miles of multiuse trails traverse a delicate ecosystem where you can see all kinds of wildlife, including seventeen species of warblers, whippoorwills, barred owls, bobwhite quails, and wild turkeys.

The park sits atop a unique piece of topography: an outcropping of serpentine stone nearly 6 miles long and 2 miles wide. It's a popular picnic destination for Chester County residents and features pavilions, informal picnic areas, play lots for kids, primitive camping sites, and recreation equipment.

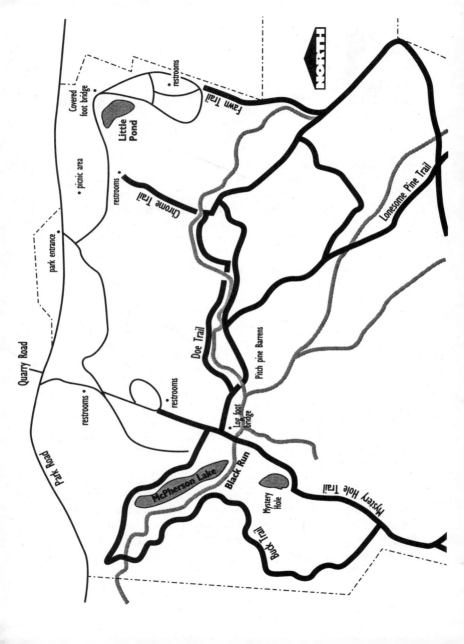

The 651-acre park is also a unique natural area of rare flora and fauna created by the stone outcropping. Half the park is pitch pine forest called barrens, where stunted growth of the trees results from the dry, acidic soil. From the mid-1800s until 1930, the area was the center of a feldspar and chromium quarrying industry. Mine openings and sinkholes throughout the park give evidence to the mining activity.

For two-wheeled adventurers, however, the park's greatest attraction is the system of trails. Two primitive campsites and two scenic overlooks are waiting to be explored by intrepid cyclists, who can ride trails with names like Buck, Mystery Hole, Lonesome Pine, Doe, Chrome, and Fawn. As you're pedaling, keep your eyes peeled for five species of rare plants, including maidenhair fern and moss pink, which are found exclusively in the barrens. And judging from some of the trail names, don't be surprised if you see a few whitetail deer on your ride!

For Further Information

Nottingham County Park (215) 932–9195.

Getting There

Nottingham Park is located approximately 30 miles southwest of Philadelphia on the U.S. 1 bypass. Take the Pennsylvania 272 Nottingham exit, turn right on Herr Drive, and follow the signs to the park entrance.

Bird-in-Hand

Mileage:	17
Approximate pedaling time:	2 hours
Terrain:	Rolling
Traffic:	While traffic is heavy on the main roads, it's light on the back roads. But stay alert for farm machinery using these roads.
Things to see:	Farmer's Market, guesthouses, bed and breakfasts, quilts for sale, Der Sonder Haus (dollhouses for sale), charming one-room schoolhouses, apple and peach orchards, the bucolic and world-famous Pennsylvania Dutch Country landscape.

Lancaster County is a bicyclist's paradise: A labyrinth of well-maintained roads with few hills extends from charming villages in all directions through the lush Pennsylvania Dutch Country.

But hold on: There's more to this historic area than effortless pedaling. Bird-in-Hand is a shopper's paradise, and this easy ride begins at the **Farmer's Market**, located in this pretty village.

Seasonal produce such as sweet corn, ripe tomatoes, green peppers, and eggplants, as well as flowers fresh off farmers' fields, fill the market stalls. The market is also a good place to buy shoofly pie and other renowned baked goods and spices such as caraway seed and sweet marjoram. Inside the market you'll also find butcher shops, cheese stands, fruit and nut stands, and dry goods and crafts for sale.

The abundance of the market reflects the rich agriculture of the

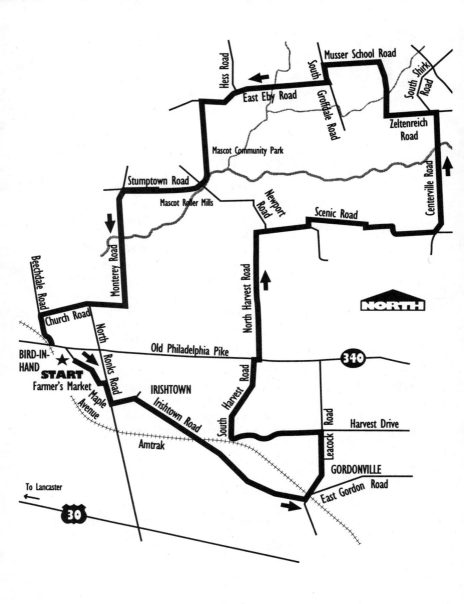

0.0   At the west end of the Farmer's Market, turn left onto Maple Avenue.

0.4   Turn right onto North Ronks Road.

0.7   Turn left onto Irishtown Road.

2.9   Turn left onto Leacock Road.

3.7   Turn left onto Harvest Drive/South Harvest Road.

5.5   Turn right onto Old Philadelphia Pike (Pennsylvania 340).

5.6   Turn left onto North Harvest Road.

6.9   Go straight through the stop sign onto Newport Road.

7.3   Turn left onto Scenic Road.

8.0   Stay on Scenic Road by making a right and a left.

8.7   Turn left onto Centerville Road.

10.0   Turn left onto Zeltenreich Road.

10.5   Turn right onto Musser School Road.

11.5   Turn left onto South Groffdale Road.

11.7   Turn right onto East Eby Road.

12.7   Turn left onto Stumptown Road.

14.7   Turn left onto Monterey Road.

15.9   Turn right onto Church Road.

16.8   Turn left onto Beechdale Road.

17.1   Turn left onto Old Philadelphia Pike (Pennsylvania 340).

17.2   Turn right into the Farmer's Market.

---

surrounding area—and the success of the Plain People who farm it. Today their population is around 70,000 and includes members of the Amish, Brethren, and Mennonite faiths.

Most of these people dress and live like the rest of society. But the most conservative groups believe in visible nonconformity as a way to preserve their beliefs and values. They compose the 35,000 or so people in Lancaster County who wear distinctive Plain clothing (dark-colored suits and broad-brimmed hats for men; modest, solid-colored dresses covered by capes and aprons for women); about 25,000 use horse-drawn vehicles.

As you ride your bike through Amish country, keep in mind that the Plain People are not actors but folks who choose to live differently. Respect their privacy, and don't interrupt their daily routine or trespass on their land. And no pictures: Many Amish believe that photographs in which they can be recognized violate biblical commandments.

Now it's time to start thinking about bikes. But first: Did you buy a packable lunch while visiting the Farmer's Market? OK—now it's time to go for a ride!

Within moments, the hustle and bustle of Pennsylvania 340 is left behind as you plunge into the traditional countryside. The narrow two-lane road leads past Groffs Greenhouse, cornfields, and farms. Just past the tourist home, there's a stop sign where you turn right onto North Ronks Road (watch for traffic). Soon you'll see Amish horse-drawn carriages and neat-as-a-pin farms.

Other sights: a Mennonite farmer painting a fence post, wooden toys for sale, dairy farms, quilts and crafts ("NO SUNDAY SALES"), birdhouses for sale, tidy orchards, and well-kept gardens filled with flowers.

For 0.1 mile you're back on Pennsylvania 340—a jarring but momentary return to the twentieth century. Then it's more gently rolling terrain (look for the house with a NO TOURISTS ALLOWED sign, views of valleys of farmhouses and silos (but not in August, when the tall corn blocks the view), quaint one-room schoolhouses (with outside pumps and outhouses), and a cemetery with headstones in German.

A good place to stop and eat the lunch you brought is **Mascot Community Park** on Stumptown Road. With picnic tables, well-manicured grounds, shade trees, and the sound of rushing water, the park is an inviting place to take a break, especially on a hot day. Upstream of the river and across Newport Road is **Mascot Roller Mills**, a restored stone gristmill. It's open Monday through Saturday, 9:00 A.M. to 4:00 P.M., May through October; tours are available.

Continuing on your bike tour around Bird-in-Hand, the charm doesn't let up: buggies stored in barns, one-lane bridges, the **Millers Store** (boasting natural foods), and garden carts for sale. Then it's back onto Pennsylvania 340 and what may seem like most of the world's traffic—but, thankfully, there's a wide shoulder for the final cruise back to the Farmer's Market.

For Further Information

Pennsylvania Dutch Convention & Visitors Bureau (717) 299–8901

Getting There

From Philadelphia drive west on U.S. 30 to the Pennsylvania Dutch Country. Bird-in-Hand is located on Pennsylvania 340, east of Lancaster. Park in the Farmer's Market on Pennsylvania 340; you can usually find a space in the busy parking lot behind the market.

Intercourse

Mileage:	16
Approximate pedaling time:	2 hours
Terrain:	Rolling
Traffic:	Heavy on Pennsylvania 340 but light on the narrow lanes that make up most of this ride. Keep an eye peeled for farm machinery using the roads as you pedal past farms.
Things to see:	People's Place Quilt Museum, Kitchen Kettle Village, Amish farms, pristine countryside

When the Amish, an austere Anabaptist sect that originated in Switzerland, settled in southeastern Pennsylvania more than 250 years ago and eventually founded this tiny village, they probably had no idea its unusual name would generate so much interest.

While no one knows for sure its origin (was it for the "entercourse" of an old racetrack or the nearby intersection of two famous roads?), one thing's for sure: It's got nothing to do with sex.

Instead, this tiny village just oozes charm. Quaint shops displaying colorful quilts for sale crowd the main street, while a constant stream of buggy traffic prevails as the local Amish go about their business.

Worth a visit is the **People's Place**, where this easy ride through lush Pennsylvania Dutch Country begins. It's a complex of shops and learning centers that also features a bookstore and a three-screen slide presentation promoting understanding of both the Amish and the Mennonite cultures that originally settled the area. The **Country**

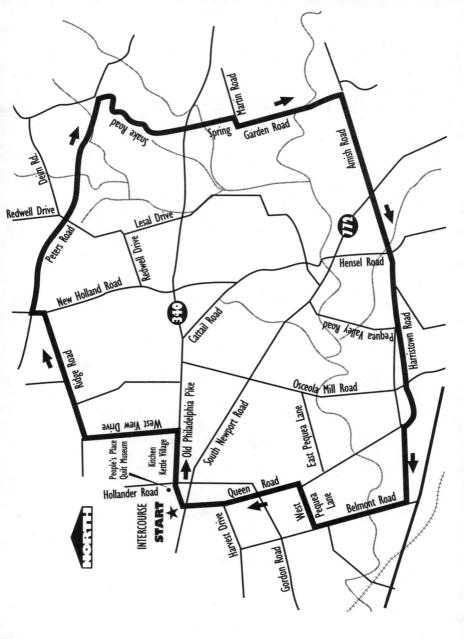

DIREC-TIONS at a glance

0.0	Turn left onto Old Philadelphia Pike (Pennsylvania 340) from the People's Place.
1.0	Turn left onto West View Drive.
2.0	Turn right onto Ridge Road.
3.4	Turn left onto New Holland Road.
3.5	Turn right onto Peters Road.
5.9	Turn right onto Snake Road.
7.1	Merge into Spring Garden Road and cross Old Philadelphia Pike (Pennsylvania 340).
7.6	Turn right onto Martin Road; then turn left onto Spring Garden Road.
8.7	Turn right onto Amish Road.
10.7	Turn right onto Harristown Road.
13.2	Turn right onto Belmont Road.
15.0	Turn right onto West Pequea Lane.
15.5	Turn left onto Queen Road.
16.0	Turn left onto South Newport Road.
16.2	Bear left onto Old Philadelphia Pike (Pennsylvania 340) in Intercourse.

Store, owned by two local Mennonite families, offers a wide selection of contemporary quilts for sale.

Quilts, as a glance at the many shops in this village quickly reveals, are a big deal in Intercourse. Here's a brief tutorial for shoppers: Traditional Lancaster County patterns include Center Diamond, Lone Star, Sunshine and Shadow, and Irish Chain. More common today are contemporary floral designs sewn in patterns of Double Wedding Ring, Crazy Quilt, Log Cabin, and Fans. Don't forget your checkbook: Contemporary full-size quilts of good quality start at around $400 and go as high as $1,000. Smaller crib quilts and wall hangings are priced lower.

But unless you're hauling a trailer behind your bike, pack your new quilt in the car before beginning this ride through the best countryside in Lancaster County. Leaving the People's Place, turn left and ride out Pennsylvania 340; at the split bear left to stay on Pennsylvania 340. Traffic is usually heavy, but there's a wide shoulder.

Soon the views change to rolling farmland, Amish farms, grapevine gardens and terraces, one-room schoolhouses, and lush greenery. Snake Lane, with its many twists and turns, is appropriately named—and a blast to ride! Back across Pennsylvania 340 look for a sign that leads to a place that does emergency repairs: GEHMAN'S BIKE SHOP—REPAIRS.

Be on the lookout for odd combinations of the quaint and the modern, such as side-by-side fields, one plowed by horse and the other by mechanical farm equipment. An ancient cemetery marks the intersection of Harristown and Belmont roads. Next there's a covered bridge on Belmont Road. Be careful as you ride up onto the bridge—gaps between the old wooden boards can catch a tire.

Don't make a wrong turn at West Pequea Lane—continue past where it comes in on the left and make the right turn when it reappears a bit farther down the road. Look for neat flower gardens in many of the well-kept yards, and watch for a stand selling wood carvings. This is Pennsylvania Dutch Country at its best!

For Further Information

Pennsylvania Dutch Convention & Visitors Bureau (717) 299–8901
Intercourse Tourist Information Center (717) 768–3882

Getting There

From Philadelphia drive west on U.S. 30 to Pennsylvania Dutch Country. Intercourse is 10 miles east of Lancaster on Pennsylvania 340.

Blue Ball

Mileage:	13
Approximate pedaling time:	1.5 hours
Terrain:	Rolling
Traffic:	Heavy on the main roads but surprisingly light on the back roads and lanes that make up the majority of this ride
Things to see:	Mennonite farms, Shady Maple Market, the delightful village of Churchtown, a covered bridge, gorgeous countryside

Located north of Pennsylvania 340 and off the well-beaten tourist path, the village of Blue Ball offers a respite from the unrelenting commercialism that marks much of Pennsylvania Dutch Country.

Which means that the emphasis in this corner of Lancaster County is on riding—not shopping, sightseeing, or educational tours. This easy and scenic ride, which begins and ends at the **Shady Maple Market** in Blue Ball, takes cyclists along narrow backroads leading through lush farmland, a pretty village, and a covered bridge. (Warning: Make sure to check for oncoming traffic before entering the dark interior of the bridge.)

As you cruise these quiet backroads, you'll notice another unique aspect to this corner of Pennsylvania Dutch Country: After horse-drawn buggies, bicycles are the most popular mode of transportation.

Why? The Mennonites who live in this part of Lancaster County prefer riding a bike to using a car for short trips. And keep an eye peeled for the latest trend, catching on fast in Amish and Mennonite communities: in-line skating.

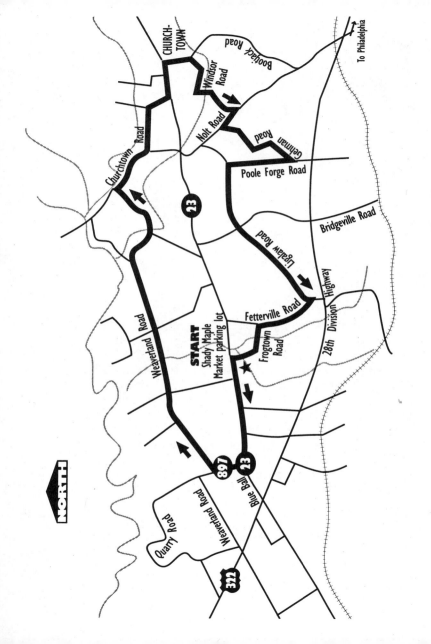

DIRECTIONS at a glance

0.0	From the Shady Maple Market parking lot, turn left and go west on Pennsylvania 23.
0.5	Turn right onto Pennsylvania 897.
0.9	Turn right onto Weaverland Road.
3.4	Bear left at the fork and descend to the covered bridge.
4.1	Turn right onto Churchtown Road.
5.9	Turn left onto Pennsylvania 23.
6.3	Turn right onto Bootjack Road.
6.5	Turn right onto Windsor Road.
7.0	Turn left onto Churchtown Road.
7.4	Turn right onto Nolt Road.
7.6	Turn left onto Gehman Road.
8.6	Turn right onto Poole Forge Road.
9.3	Turn left onto Ligalaw Road.
11.3	Turn right onto Fetterville Road.
11.9	Turn left onto Frogtown Road.
12.5	Turn left onto Pennsylvania 23 and return to Shady Maple Market.

It's all part of the religious heritage of the Plain People: The conveniences that the "English," or non-Amish, world takes for granted are seen as tempting forces that undermine the family. As a result, many of the Amish don't use electricity, drive cars, or have telephones. They farm with horse-drawn equipment, travel in horse-drawn buggies, and use propane gas stoves and refrigerators, oil lamps, and clothes washers powered by gas engines or compressed air. Needless to say, wheels are OK—whether on straight-out-of-the-1930s push scooters, bikes, or in-line skates.

About halfway through this ride, the neat farmland gives way to the village of Churchtown, which lives up to its name with a large number of churches, as well as several antiques and gift shops. The **Churchtown Inn**, a bed and breakfast, is a restored 1735 fieldstone mansion that overlooks an Amish farm. After Churchtown more

farms, pretty homesteads, and tidy gardens make up the rest of the ride, which ends at Shady Maple Market.

Shady Maple Market is a great place to finish a ride, especially if you've worked up a big appetite. Warning: Members of local bike clubs frequent the Shady Maple Smorgasbord on their regular club rides—and have to be careful about eating too much! It's a great place to eat, whether before the ride or after.

For Further Information

Pennsylvania Dutch Convention & Visitors Bureau (717) 299–8901

Getting There

The Pennsylvania Dutch Country is located west of Philadelphia along U.S. 30. Blue Ball is on Pennsylvania 23, east of the intersection of Pennsylvania 23 and U.S. 322. The Shady Maple Market features a large lot where you can park your car.

17TH PENNSYLVANIA CAVALRY.
2D BRIGADE, 1ST DIVISION, CAVALRY CORPS, ARMY OF THE POTOMAC.

Gettysburg National Military Park

Mileage:	7.4
Approximate pedaling time:	1 hour
Terrain:	Gently rolling
Traffic:	Generally light, but watch for tour buses near the parking areas
Things to see:	Civil War monuments and historical markers, beautiful countryside, old stone walls, the National Cemetery, Eisenhower National Historic Site

Whether you've come to tour this famous battlefield by car, foot, or bicycle, it's hard to avoid a feeling of melancholia that comes from an understanding of the enormity of what happened here on three hot days in July 1863.

But come here just the same, and be sure to explore Gettysburg National Military Park on a bike: Touring on two wheels is the best way to understand the human dimensions of this crucial Civil War battle.

Still, like other visitors, people touring by bike should begin in the visitor center, with its excellent museum that provides a solid overview of the events of 1863 that led up to the battle. But don't expect to be bombarded with a lot of confusing military facts and figures. Exhibits featuring haversacks and hardtack, hot wool uniforms shredded by musket fire, and flags lost and won on the field add a human—and sometimes gruesome—perspective to your visit.

What *did* happen in these fields and woods outside this Pennsylvania hamlet in 1863? Simply put, the Confederate tide was pushed back for the second and final time by the wall of determined men who made up the Union forces.

In effect, the Southern cause was lost in these fields. And the cost

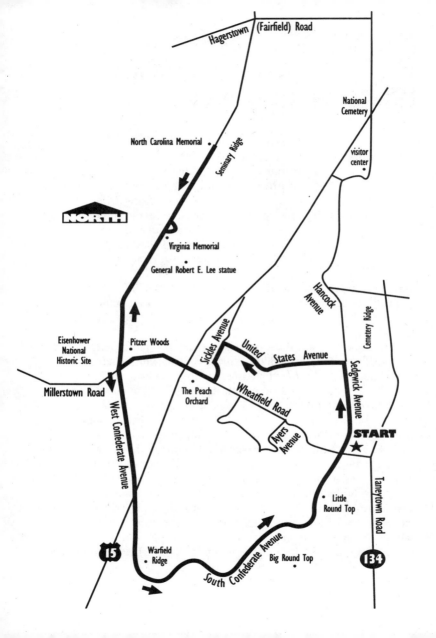

DIREC-TIONS at a glance

0.0	From Wheatfield Road, turn right onto Sedgwick Avenue.
0.5	Turn left onto United States Avenue (the DO NOT ENTER sign is for the auto tour traffic and does not apply to bicyclists).
1.2	Turn left onto Sickles Avenue.
1.45	Turn right onto Millerstown Road.
1.6	Go straight across Business Route U.S. 15.
1.94	Turn right onto West Confederate Avenue.
3.29	Turn around at North Carolina Memorial.
5.38	Go straight across Business Route U.S. 15.
7.4	Turn right onto Wheatfield Road parking area.

in human lives and suffering was enormous: When the fighting ended on July 3, 1863, casualties from both armies totaled more than 50,000 men. It was the largest armed conflict fought in the Western Hemisphere.

After picking up a copy of the battlefield map that shows the bike tour, begin your ride from the visitor center by pedaling south on Pennsylvania 134 (Taneytown Road) to Wheatfield Road and turn right. (You can also drive to this point and park.)

Touring the battlefield on a bicycle gives you a distinct advantage over the millions of visitors who see it through the windshield of the family car or the window of a tour bus. For one thing, pedaling makes you feel wonderfully alive, a nice contrast to the grim events of more than a century ago.

Further, markers and monuments along the route are much more accessible by bike: You're not as likely to drive by an intriguing spot as when touring by car, with the endless hassle of parking, getting out, and getting back in. On a bike the wind is in your hair, you smell the fields and woods of the rolling Pennsylvania countryside, and the effort of riding up the easy hills makes you feel alive; all of this contributes to the experience.

If you're touring by fat-tired bike, so much the better. On a sturdy mountain bike, it's easy to peel off across the flat, stony fields to examine monuments, gun emplacements, markers, fences, and old stone walls that otherwise would seem too far away.

If the pleasures of exploring Gettysburg by bike sound low-key, you're right: The scenery consists of modest vistas of surrounding fields, woods, stone walls, and, in the spring, clusters of forget-me-nots. You'll spend much of your time reading inscriptions on monuments and statues. Often the quiet and peacefulness impart a feeling of solitude.

Of course, one reason for the sense of introspection Gettysburg imparts is its history. And while students of the events that took place here 130 years ago can bone up at the visitor center on the fine details of the battle, casual visitors on a bike need only pedal to come face to face with the battle's momentous events.

The **Virginia Memorial**, with its huge statue of General Robert E. Lee astride his horse, commemorates one such event. The field to the east is the site of Pickett's Charge, the last Confederate assault of the battle. From this spot General Lee watched 12,000 of his Confederate troops march across 1 mile of open field toward the Federal line. The attack was as spectacular as it was doomed: Soon 8,000 soldiers lay dead in the field.

Or **Little Round Top**, with its commanding view of the battlefield. The area saw some of the fiercest fighting on the second day of the battle. Like **Seminary Ridge** and **Cemetery Ridge**, Little Round Top is former molten rock that flowed into the red sandstones and shales of the Gettysburg Valley 180 million years ago. The sedimentary rock wore away, leaving these harder rock features that served as major sites during the battle.

At the **National Cemetery**, north of the visitor center, you can see where Abraham Lincoln read his Gettysburg Address at the cemetery's dedication on November 19, 1863. While the speech is widely regarded as one the greatest orations in history, it almost didn't happen: Lincoln had been invited to the cemetery's dedication as an afterthought. In the style of the day, the main speaker addressed the crowd for two hours before the president spoke. Later Lincoln remarked that his own two-minute speech "fell like a wet blanket" over the audience.

When is the best season to ride a bike at Gettysburg? Spring, with blooming wildflowers and verdant fields, is a popular time to visit. Yet beware: It's also when school buses filled with rambunctious children descend on the battlefield. Fall, with its crisp, cool temperatures and turning leaves, may be better. The riot of color usually begins in mid-October.

If you visit in the summer, try to plan your ride for the early morning or evening hours: July and August in south-central Pennsylvania are usually hot and humid.

How did the events that happened here in 1863 turn out? Although the Civil War ground on for another two years after the Battle of Gettysburg ended, the Southern cause was effectively lost here. The day after the battle ended, Union troops celebrated their best Fourth of July since the war began, and Lee commenced his long retreat back to Virginia.

Your visit to Gettysburg, however, will end with a greater understanding of the historic events that took place here and with rich insights into the huge scale of human suffering that occurred here in 1863—all because you toured Gettysburg on a bike.

For Further Information

Gettysburg Travel Council (717) 334–6274
Gettysburg National Military Park (717) 334–1124

Getting There

Gettysburg is located on U.S. 30 in south-central Pennsylvania between York and Chambersburg, about a two-and-a-half-hour drive from Philadelphia, one way. The Gettysburg Battlefield Visitors Center is on Pennsylvania 134, 1 mile south of town.

Bicycling Clubs

International

International Mountain Bicycling Association
Box 412043
Los Angeles, CA 90041

National

Bikecentennial
P.O. Box 8308
Missoula, MO 59807

League of American Wheelmen
190 West Ostend Street, Suite 120
Baltimore, MD 21230-3731

Pennsylvania

Bicycle Club of Philadelphia
P.O. Box 30235
Philadelphia, PA 19103

Brandywine Bicycle Club
P.O. Box 3162
West Chester, PA 19381

Bucks County Biking
P.O. Box 534
New Hope, PA 18938
(215) 862–0733

Central Bucks Bicycle Club
P.O. Box 295
Buckingham, PA 18912
(215) 348–5679

Cycling Enthusiasts of Delaware Valley
9325 Marsden Street
Philadelphia, PA 19114
(215) 338–9159

Delaware Valley Bicycle Club
P.O. Box 274
Drexel Hill, PA 19026
(215) 735–5781

Suburban Cyclists Unlimited
P.O. Box 401
Horsham, PA 19044

Bicycle Shops

Here is a brief list of a few of the many bicycle shops found in and around Philadelphia. Remember that businesses come and go, so it's a good idea to call ahead. This list is completely arbitrary and by no means exhaustive; nor does it constitute any endorsement by the authors or publisher.

Philadelphia

Jay's Pedal Power Bikes
512 East Girard Avenue
Philadelphia, PA
(215) 425–5111

The Wall
4342 Main Street, Manayunk
Philadelphia, PA 19127
(215) 482–9972

Delaware County

Cycles BiKyle
1044 Lancaster Avenue
Bryn Mawr, PA 19010
(215) 525–8442

Montgomery County

R.E.I.
200 West Ridge Pike
Conshohocken, PA
(215) 940–0809

Chester County

Bike Line
711 Nutt Road (Pennsylvania 23)
Phoenixville, PA 19460
(215) 935-9111

Bike Line
200 West Gay Street
West Chester, PA 19380
(215) 436–8984

Downingtown Bicycle Shop
833 West Lancaster Avenue (Business Route 30)
Downingtown, PA 19335
(215) 269–5626

Bucks County

Bike Line
Mercer Square Shopping Center
73 Old Dublin Pike
Doylestown, PA 18091
(215) 348–8015

Bike Line
298 York Road
Warminster, PA 18974
(215) 675–1739

Guy's Bicycles
326 East Street Road
Feasterville, PA 19053
(215) 355–1166

Kiddle Cyclery & Ski Chalet
Route 413, P.O. Box 295
Buckingham, PA 18912
(215) 794–8958

Newtown Bicycle Shop
102 South State Street
Newtown, PA 18940
(215) 968–3200

Lancaster County

Bicycle World
747 South Broad Street (Pennsylvania 501)
Lititz, PA 17602
(215) 626–0650

Adams County

Gettysburg Schwinn
100 Buford Avenue
Gettysburg, PA 17325
(717) 334–7791